Multicore Software
Development Techniques

Multicore Software Development Techniques

Applications, Tips, and Tricks

Rob Oshana

ELSEVIER

AMSTERDAM • BOSTON • HEIDELBERG • LONDON
NEW YORK • OXFORD • PARIS • SAN DIEGO
SAN FRANCISCO • SINGAPORE • SYDNEY • TOKYO

Newnes is an imprint of Elsevier

Newnes

Newnes is an imprint of Elsevier
The Boulevard, Langford Lane, Kidlington, Oxford OX5 1GB, UK
225 Wyman Street, Waltham, MA 02451, USA

ISBN: 978-0-12-800958-1

British Library Cataloguing-in-Publication Data
A catalogue record for this book is available from the British Library

Library of Congress Cataloging-in-Publication Data
A catalog record for this book is available from the Library of Congress

For information on all Newnes publications
visit our website at http://store.elsevier.com/

Working together
to grow libraries in
developing countries

This book is dedicated to my family, Susan, Sam, and Noah.

CONTENTS

CHAPTER 1

Principles of Parallel Computing

A multicore processor is a computing device that contains two or more independent processing elements (referred to as "cores") integrated on to a single device, that read and execute program instructions. There are many architectural styles of multicore processors, and many application areas, such as embedded processing, graphics processing, and networking.

There are many factors driving multicore adoption:

- Increases in mobile traffic
- Increases in communication between multiple devices
- Increase in semiconductor content (e.g., automotive increases in semiconductor content are driving automotive manufacturers to consider multicore to improve affordability, "green" technology, safety, and connectivity, see Figure 1.1)

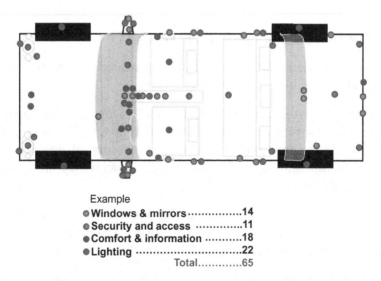

Example
- Windows & mirrors ·············14
- Security and access ···········11
- Comfort & information ··········18
- Lighting ····························22
                              Total·········65

Figure 1.1 Semiconductor content in automotive is increasing.

Multicore Software Development Techniques. DOI: http://dx.doi.org/10.1016/B978-0-12-800958-1.00001-2

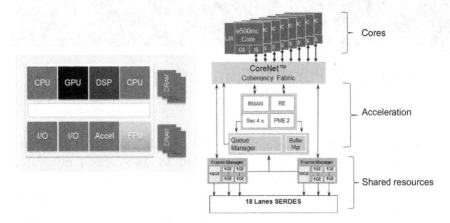

Figure 1.2 A generic multicore system (left) and an example multicore device from industry (right).

A typical multicore processor will have multiple cores which can be the same (homogeneous) or different (heterogeneous) accelerators (the more generic term is "processing element") for dedicated functions such as video or network acceleration, as well as a number of shared resources (memory, cache, peripherals such as ethernet, display, codecs, UART, etc.) (Figure 1.2)

1.1 CONCURRENCY VERSUS PARALLELISM

There are important differences between concurrency and parallelism as they relate to multicore processing.

Concurrency: A condition that exists when at least two software tasks are making progress, although at different times. This is a more generalized form of parallelism that can include time-slicing as a form of virtual parallelism. Systems that support concurrency are designed for interruptability.

Parallelism: A condition that arises when at least two threads are executing simultaneously. Systems that support parallelism are designed for independentability, such as a multicore system.

A program designed to be concurrent may or may not be run in parallel; concurrency is more an attribute of a program, parallelism may occur when it executes (see Figure 1.3).

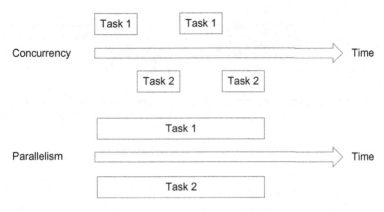

Figure 1.3 Concurrency versus parallelism.

It is time to introduce an algorithm that should be memorized when thinking about multicore systems. Here it is:

High-performance = parallelism + memory hierarchy − contention

- "Parallelism" is all about exposing parallelism in the application
- "Memory hierarchy" is all about maximizing data locality in the network, disk, RAM, cache, core, etc.
- "Contention" is all about minimizing interactions between cores (e.g., locking, synchronization, etc.)

To achieve the best HPC or "High Peformance Computing" result, to get the best performance we need to get the best possible parallelism, use memory efficiently, and reduce the contention. As we move forward we will touch on each of these areas.

1.2 SYMMETRIC AND ASYMMETRIC MULTIPROCESSING

Efficiently allocating resources in multicore systems can be a challenge. Depending on the configuration, the multiple software components in these systems may or may not be aware of how other components are using these resources. There are two primary forms of multiprocessing, as shown in Figure 1.4;

- Symmetric multiprocessing
- Asymmetric multiprocessing

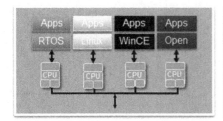 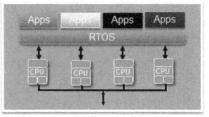

Figure 1.4 Asymmetric multiprocessing (left) and symmetric multiprocessing (right).

1.2.1 Symmetric Multiprocessing

Symmetric multiprocessing (SMP) uses a single copy of the operating system on all of the system's cores. The operating system has visibility into all system element, and can allocate resources on the multiple cores with little or no guidance from the application developer. SMP dynamically allocates resources to specific applications rather than to cores which leads to greater utilization of available processing power. Key characteristics of SMP include:

A collection of homogeneous cores with a common view of system resources such as sharing a coherent memory space and using CPUs that communicate using a large coherent memory space.

Applicable for general purpose applications or applications that may not be entirely known at design time. Applications that my need to suspend because of memory accesses or may need to migrate or restart on any core fit into a SMP model as well. Multithreaded applications are SMP friendly.

1.2.2 Asymmetric Multiprocessing

AMP can be:

* *homogeneous*—each CPU runs the same type and version of the operating system
* *heterogeneous*—each CPU runs either a different operating system or a different version of the same operating system

In heterogeneous systems, you must either implement a proprietary communications scheme or choose two OSs that share a common

API and infrastructure for interprocessor communications. There must be well-defined and implemented methods for accessing shared resources.

In an AMP system, an application process will always runs on the same CPU, even when other CPUs run idle. This can lead to one CPU being under- or overutilized. In some cases it may be possible to migrate a process dynamically from one CPU to another. There may be side effects of doing this, such as requiring checkpointing of state information or a service interruption when the process is halted on one CPU and restarted on another CPU. This is further complicated if the CPUs run different operating systems.

In AMP systems, the processor cores communicate using large coherent bus memories, shared local memories, hardware FIFOS, and other direct connections.

AMP is better applied to known data-intensive applications where it is better at maximizing efficiency for every task in the system such as audio and video processing. AMP is not as good as a pool of general computing resources.

The key reason there are AMP multicore devices is because it is the most economical way to deliver multiprocessing to specific tasks. The performance, energy, and area envelope is much better than SMP.

Table 1.1 is a summary of SMP and AMP multicore systems.

Table 1.1 Comparison of SMP and AMP		
Feature	SMP	AMP
Dedicated processor by function	No	Yes
Legacy application migration	In most cases	Yes
Intercore messaging	Fast (OS primitives)	Slow (application)
Load balancing	Yes	No
Seamless resource sharing	Yes	No
Scalable beyond dual CPU	Yes	Limited
Mixed OS environment	No	Yes
Thread synchronization between CPU's	Yes	No

1.3 PARALLELISM SAVES POWER

Multicore reduces average power comsumption. It is becoming harder to achieve increased processor performance from traditional techniques such as increasing the clock frequency or developing new architectural approaches to increase instructions per cycle (IPC). Frequency scaling of CPU cores is no longer valid, primarily due to power challenges.

An electronic circuit has a capacitance, C, associated with it. Capacitance is the ability of a circuit to store energy. This can be defined as;

$$C = \text{charge (q)}/\text{voltage (V)},$$

And the charge on a circuit can therefore be $q = CV$

Work can be defined as the act of pushing something (charge) across a "distance." In this discussion we can define this in electrostatic terms as pushing the charge, q from 0 to V volts in a circuit.

$$W = V*q, \text{ or in other terms, } W = V*CV \text{ or } W = CV^2$$

Power is defined as work over time, or in this discussion it is how many times a second we oscillate the circuit.

$P = (\text{work})W/(\text{time})T$ and since $T = 1/F$ then $P = WF$ or substituting,

$P = CV^2F$

We can use an example to reflect this. Assuming the circuit in Figure 1.5.

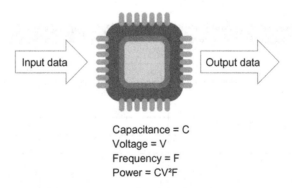

Capacitance = C
Voltage = V
Frequency = F
Power = CV²F

Figure 1.5 A simple circuit.

This simple circuit has a capacitance C, a Voltage V, a frequency F, and therefore a Power defined as $P = CV^2F$

If we instead use a multicore circuit as shown in Figure 1.6, we can make the following assumptions;

- We will use two cores instead of one
- We will clock this circuit as half the frequency for each of the two cores
- We will use more circuitry (capacitance C) with two cores instead of one, plus some additional circuitry to manage these cores, assume $2.1 \times$ the capacitance
- By reducing the frequency, we can also reduce the voltage across the circuit, assume we can use a voltage of 0.7 or the single core circuit (it could be half the single core circuit but lets assume a bit more for additional overhead)

Given these assumptions, the Power can be defined as

$$P = CV^2F = (2.1)(0.7)^2(0.5) = 0.5145$$

What this says is by going from one core to multicore we can reduce overall power consumption by over 48%, given the conservative assumptions above.

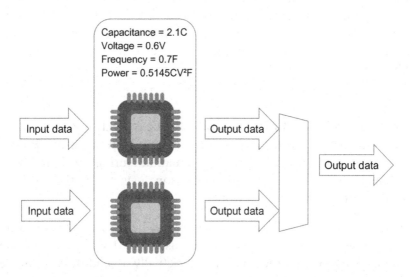

Capacitance = 2.1C
Voltage = 0.6V
Frequency = 0.7F
Power = 0.5145CV²F

Input data

Output data

Output data

Input data

Output data

Figure 1.6 A parallel multicore circuit.

There are other benefits from going to multicore. When we can use several smaller simpler cores instead of one big complicated core, we can achieve more predictable performance and achieve a simpler programming model in some cases.

1.3.1 Limit: "Hidden Parallelism" Gains are Slowing Down

Application performance has been increasing by 52% per year as measured by SpecInt benchmarks. This performance was due to transistor density improvements and architectural changes such as improvements in Instruction Level Parallelism (ILP)

Superscalar designs provided many forms of parallelism not visible to programmer, such as

- multiple instruction issue done by the hardware (advances in VLIW architectures support multiple instruction issue using an optimizing compiler)
- dynamic scheduling: hardware discovers parallelism between instructions
- speculative execution: look past predicted branches
- nonblocking caches: multiple outstanding memory ops

The good thing for the software developer is that these architectural improvements did not require the software developer to do anything different or unique, all of the work was done by the hardware. But in the past decade or so, there have been few significant changes to keep promoting this performance improvement further.

1.3.2 Another Limit: Chip Yield and Process Technologies

Semiconductor process technologies are getting very expensive. Process technologies continue to improve but manufacturing costs and yield problems limit use of density. As fabrication costs go up, the yield (the percentage of usable devices) drops.

This is another place where parallelism can help. Generally speaking, more smaller, simpler processors are easier to design and validate. Using many of these at the same time is actually a valid business model used by several multicore vendors.

1.3.3 Another Limit: Basic Laws of Physics and the Speed of Light

Data needs to travel some distance, r, to get from memory to the CPU. So to get one data element per cycle, this means 10^{12} times per second at the speed of light, $c = 3 \times 10^8$ m/s. Thus $r < c/10^{12} = 0.3$ mm.

If our goal is lets say 1 teraflop, then we need to put 1 Tbyte of storage in a 0.3 mm × 0.3 mm area. At this area, each bit must occupy about 1 square Angstrom, or the size of a small atom. Obviously this is not possible today so we have no choice but to move to parallelism.

Also keep in mind that chip density is continuing to increase ~2 × every 2 years, but the clock speed is not. So what is the solution? Well we need to double the number of processor cores instead. If you believe that there is little or no hidden parallelism (ILP) to be found, then parallelism must be exposed to and managed by software.

1.4 KEY CHALLENGES OF PARALLEL COMPUTING

Parallel computing does have some challenges. The key challenges of parallel and multicore computing can be summarized as follows;

1. Finding enough parallelism
2. Achieving the right level of Granularity
3. Exploiting Locality in computation
4. Proper Load balancing
5. Coordination and synchronization

All of these things makes parallel programming more challenging than sequential programming. Lets take a look at each of of these.

1.4.1 Finding Enough Parallelism

A computer program always has a sequential part and a parallel part. What does this mean? Lets start with a simple example below.

```
1. A = B + C
2. D = A + 2
3. E = D + A
4. For (i = 0; i < E; i++)
5.     N(i) = 0;
```

In this example, steps 1, 2 and 4 are "sequential." There is a data dependence that prevents these three instructions from executing in parallel.

Steps 4 and 5 are parallel. There is no data dependence and multiple iterations of N(i) can execute in parallel.

Even with E a large number, say 200, the best we can do is to sequentially execute 4 instructions, no matter how many processors we have available to us.

Multicore architectures have sensitivity to the structure of software. In general, parallel execution incurs overheads that limit the expected execution time benefits that can be achieved. Performance improvements therefore depend on the software algorithms and their implementations. In some cases, parallel problems can achieve speedup factors close to the number of cores, or potentially more if the problem is split up to fit within each core's cache(s), which avoids the use of the much slower main system memory. However, as we will show, many applications cannot be accelerated adequately unless the application developer spends a significant effort to refactor the portions of the application.

As an example, we can think of an application as having both sequential parts and parallel parts as shown in Figure 1.7.

This application, when executed on a single core processor, will execute sequentially and take a total of 12 time units to complete (Figure 1.8).

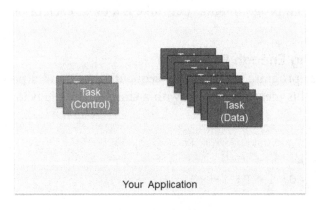

Figure 1.7 An application showing sequential (control) parts and data (parallel) parts.

Task (Control)	Task (Control)	Task (Data)	Task (Data)	Task (Data)	Task (Data)	Task (Data)	Task (Data)	Task (Data)	Task (Data)	Task (Data)	Task (Data)

Figure 1.8 Execution on a single core processor, 12 total time units.

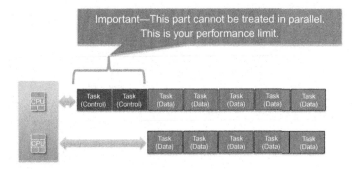

Figure 1.9 Execution on a two core multicore processor, 7 total time units.

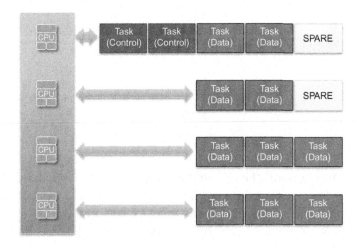

Figure 1.10 Execution on a four core multicore processor, 5 total time units.

If we run this same application on a dual core processor (Figure 1.9), the application will take a total of 7 time units, limited by the sequential part of the code that cannot execute in parallel due to reasons we showed earlier.

This is a speedup of $12/7 = 1.7 \times$ from the single core processor.

If we take this further to a four core system (Figure 1.10), we can see a total execution time of 5 units for a total speedup of $12/5 = 2.4 \times$ from the single core processor and $7/5 = 1.4 \times$ over the 2 core system.

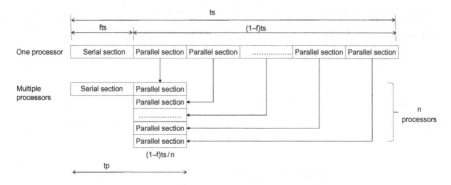

Figure 1.11 General solution of multicore scalability.

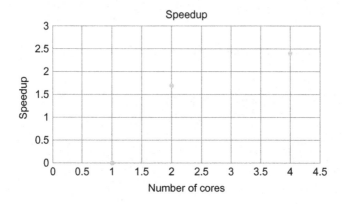

Figure 1.12 Speedup trend (# cores versus speedup).

If the fraction of the computation that cannot be divided into concurrent tasks is f, and no overhead incurs when the computation is divided into concurrent parts, the time to perform the computation with n processors is given by $t_p \geq ft_s + [(1 - f)t_s]/n$, as shown in Figure 1.11.

If we use the results from the above example and plot speedup versus number of cores, we get the plot shown in Figure 1.12.

The general solution to this is called "Amdahl's Law" and is shown in Figure 1.13.

Amdahl's Law states that parallel performance is limited by the portion of serial code in the algorithm. Specifically:

$$\text{Speedup} = 1/(S + (1 - S)/N)$$

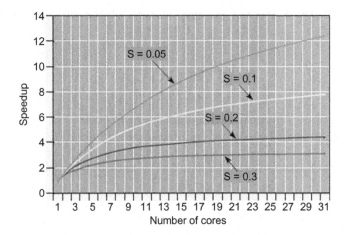

Figure 1.13 Amdahl's Law.

where S is the portion of the algorithm running serialized code and N is the number of processors running parallelized code.

Amdahl's Law implies that adding additional cores results in additional overheads and latencies. These overheads and latencies serialize execution between communicating and noncommunicating cores by requiring mechanisms such as hardware barriers, resource contention, etc. There are also various interdependent sources of latency and overhead due to processor architecture (e.g., cache coherency), system latencies and overhead (e.g., processor scheduling), and application latencies and overhead (e.g., synchronization).

Parallelism overhead comes from areas such as;

- Overhead from starting a thread or process
- Overhead of communicating shared data
- Overhead of synchronizing
- Overhead from extra (redundant) computation required to parallelize some parallel algorithms

Of couse Amdahl's Law is sensitive to application workloads (e.g., data dependencies) and predicts that as the number of cores increase, the size of the overheads and latencies increases as well.

Lets look at a couple more quick examples:

Assume 95% of a program's execution time occurs inside a loop that can be executed in parallel. What is the maximum speedup we should expect from a parallel version of the program executing on 8 CPUs?

$$\text{Speedup} = \frac{1}{S + \frac{1-S}{N}}$$

S = Portion of algorithm running serialized code
N = Number of Processors running serialized code

95% program's execution time can be executed in parallel

8 CPUs

S = 1 − 0.95 = 0.05
N = 8

$$\text{Speedup} = \frac{1}{0.05 + \frac{1-0.05}{8}}$$

Speedup = 5.9

Assume 5% of a parallel program's execution time is spent within inherently sequential code. What is the maximum speedup achievable by this program, regardless of how many processing elements are used?

$$\text{Speedup} = \frac{1}{S + \frac{1-S}{N}}$$

5% parallel program's execution time is spent within inherently sequential code

N = ∞

$$\text{Speedup} = \frac{1}{0.05 + \frac{1-0.05}{N}} = \frac{1}{0.05} = 20$$

Given the impact of these latencies and overhead, the application developer tuning focus must change to reducing or eliminating these sources of latency as we will see later.

There are some inherent limmitations to Amdahl's Law. Its proof focuses on the steps in a particular algorithm, but does not consider whether other algorithms with more parallelism may exist. As an application developer, one should always consider refactoring algorithms to make them more parallel if possible. Amdahl's Law also focused on "fixed" problem sizes such as the processing of a video frame, where simply adding more cores will eventually have diminishing returns due to the extra communication overhead incurred as the number of cores increases.

There are other models, such as Gustafson's Law which models a multicore system where the proportion of the computations that are sequential normally decreases as the problem size increases. In other words, for a system where the problem size is not fixed, the performance increases can continue to grow by adding more processors. For example for a networking application which inputs TCP/IP network packets, additional cores will allow for more and more network packets to be processed with very little additional overhead as the number of packets increases.

Gustafson's Law states that "Scaled Speedup" $= N + (1 - N) \times S$, where S is the serial portion of the algorithm running parallelized and N is the number of processors. You can see from Figure 1.14 that the curves do not flatten out as severely as Amdahl's Law.

This limitation then leads to a tradeoff that the application developer needs to understand. In each application, the important algorithm need sufficiently large units of work to run fast in parallel (i.e., large granularity), but not so large that there is not enough parallel work to perform.

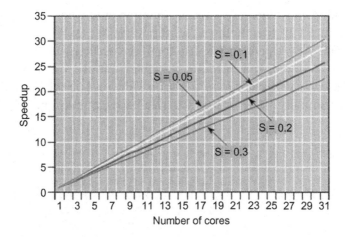

Figure 1.14 Gustafson's Law.

1.4.2 Data Dependencies

Lets spend a bit more time on data dependencies.

When algorithms are implemented serially, there is a well-defined operation order which can be very inflexible. In the edge detection example, for a given data block, the Sobel cannot be computed until after the smoothing function completes. For other sets of operations, such as within the correction function, the order in which pixels are corrected may be irrelevant.

Dependencies between data reads and writes determine the partial order of computation. There are three types of data dependencies which limit the ordering: true data dependencies, antidependencies, and output dependencies (Figure 1.15).

True data dependencies imply an ordering between operations in which a data value may not be read until after its value has been written. These are fundamental dependencies in an algorithm, although it might be possible to refactor algorithms to minimize the impact of this data dependency.

Antidependencies have the opposite relationship and can possibly be resolved by variable renaming. In an antidependency, a data value cannot be written until the previous data value has been read. In Figure 1.15, the final assignment to A cannot occur before B is assigned, because B needs the previous value of A. In the final assignment, variable A is renamed to D, then the B and D assignments may be reordered.

Renaming may increase storage requirements when new variables are introduced if the lifetimes of the variables overlap as code is parallelized. Antidependencies are common occurrences in sequential code. For example, intermediate variables defined outside the loop may be used within each loop iteration. This is fine when operations occur sequentially. The same variable storage may be repeatedly

Data dependency	Anti-dependency	Output dependency
A = 4 * C + 3; B = A + 1; A = 3 * C + 4;	A = 4 * C + 3; B = A + 1; A = 3 * C + 4;	A = 4 * C + 3; B = A + 1; A = 3 * C + 4;
Read after write	Write after read	Write after write

Figure 1.15 Key data dependencies that limit parallelism.

reused. However, when using shared memory, if all iterations were run in parallel, they would be competing for the same shared intermediate variable space. One solution would be to have each iteration use its own local intermediate variables. Minimizing variable lifetimes through proper scoping helps to avoid these dependency types.

The third type of dependency is an output dependency. In an output dependency, writes to a variable may not be reordered if they change the final value of the variable that remains when the instructions are complete. In Figure 1.15c, the final assignment to A may not be moved above the first assignment, because the remaining value will not be correct.

Parallelizing an algorithm requires both honoring dependencies and appropriately matching the parallelism to the available resources. Algorithms with a high amount of data dependencies will not parallelize effectively. When all antidependencies are removed and still partitioning does not yield acceptable performance, consider changing algorithms to find an equivalent result using an algorithm which is more amenable to parallelism. This may not be possible when implementing a standard with strictly prescribed algorithms. In other cases, there may be effective ways to achieve similar results.

Data dependencies fundamentally order the code.

Discuss three main types

Analyze code to see where critical dependencies are and if they can be removed or must be honored

Parallel dependencies are *usually not so local*—rather between tasks or iterations.

Lets take a look at some examples;

Loop nest 1

```
for(i = 0; i < n; i + + ){
    a[i] = a[i − 1] + b[i]
}
```

```
Loop 1: a [0] = a [− 1] + b [0]
Loop 2: a [1] = a [0] + b [1]
......
Loop N: a [N] = a [N − 1] + b [N]
```

Here, Loop 2 is dependent on result of Loop 1: To compute a [1], one needs a [0] which can be obtained from Loop 1. Hence, Loop nest 1 cannot be parallelized because there is a loop carried dependence flow on the other loop.

Loop nest 2

$$for(i = 0; i < n; i + +){$$
$$a[i] = a[i] + b[i]$$
$$}$$

```
Loop 1: a[0] = a[0] + b[0]
Loop 2: a[1] = a[1] + b[1]
......
Loop N: a[N] = a[N] + b[N]
```

Here, Loop nest 2 can be parallelized because the antidependence from the read of a [i] to the write of a [i] has an (=) direction and it is not loop carried.

Loop nest 3

$$for(i = 0; i < n; i + +){$$
$$a[4*i] = a[2*i - i]$$
$$}$$

```
Loop 1: a[0] = a[-1]
Loop 2: a[4] = a[1]
......
Loop N: a[4*N] = a[2*N - 1]
```

We can see that there is no dependency between any loops in Loop nest 3. Hence, Loop nest 3 can b parallelized.

1.4.3 Achieving the Right Level of Granularity

Granularity can be described as the ratio of computation to communication in a parallel program. There are two types of granularity as shown in Figure 1.16;

Fine-grained parallelism implies partitioning the application into small amounts of work done leading to a low computation to communication ratio. For example, if we partition a "for" loop into independent parallel computions by unrolling the loop, this would be an example of fine-grained parallelism. One of the downsides to fine-grained parallelism is that there may be many synchronization points,

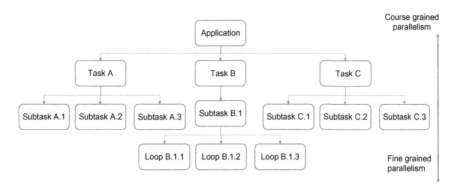

Figure 1.16 Course-grained and fine-grained parallelism.

for example, the compiler will insert synchronization points after each loop iteration, that may cause additional overhead. Also, many loop iterations would have to be parallelized in order to get decent speedup, but the developer has more control over load balancing the application.

Coarse-grained parallelism is where there is a high computation to communication ratio. For example, if we partition an application into several high level tasks that then get allocated to different cores, this would be an example of coarse-grained parallelism. The advantage of this is that there is more parallel code running at any point in time and there are fewer synchronizations required. However, load balancing may not be ideal as the higher level tasks are usually not all equivalent as far as execution time.

Lets take one more example. Lets say we want to multiply each element of an array, A by a vector X (Figure 1.17). Lets think about how to decompose this problem into the right level of granularity. The code for something like this would look like:

```
for (i = 0, N − 1)
  for (j = 0, N − 1)
    y[i] = A[I,j] * x[j];
```

From this algorithm we can see that each output element of y depends on one row of A and all of x. All tasks are of the same size in terms of number of operations.

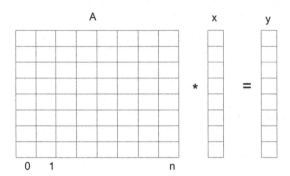

Figure 1.17 Matrix multiplication with a vector.

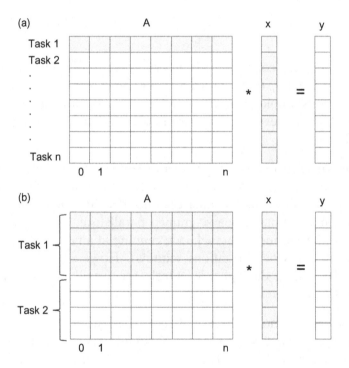

Figure 1.18 (a) Fine-grained parallelism. (b) Course-grained parallelism.

How can we break this into tasks? Course-grained with a smaller number of tasks or fine-grained with a larger number of tasks. Figure 1.18 shows an example of each.

1.4.4 Locality and Parallelism
As you may know from your introductory computer architecture courses in college, large memories are slow, fast memories are small

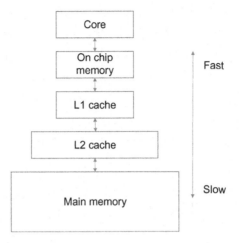

Figure 1.19 Memory hierarchies.

(Figure 1.19). The slow accesses to "remote" data we can generalize as "communication."

In general, storage hierarchies are large and fast. Most multicore processors have large, fast caches. Of course, our multicore algorithms should do most work on local data closer to the core.

Lets first discuss how data is accessed. In order to improve performance in a multicore system (or any system for that matter) we should strive for these two goals:

1. Data reuse: when possible reuse the same or nearby data used multiple times. This approach is mainly Intrinsic in computation
2. Data locality: with this approach the goal is for data to be reused and to be present in "fast memory" like a cache. Take advantage of the same data or the same data transfer

Computations that have reuse can achieve locality using appropriate data placement and layout and with intelligent Code reordering and transformations.

Some common cache terminology can now be reviewed:

- Cache hit: this is an in-cache memory access and from a computation perspective is "cheap" in the sense that the access time is generally only one cycle
- Cache miss: this is a noncached memory access and are computationally "expensive" in the sense that multiple cycles are required to

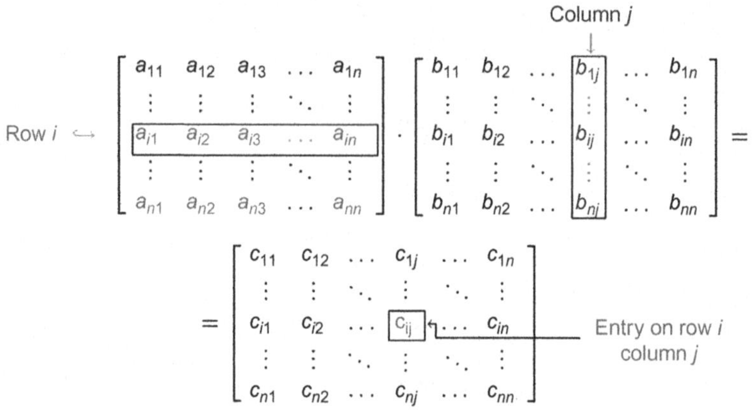

Column j

$$\begin{bmatrix} a_{11} & a_{12} & a_{13} & \cdots & a_{1n} \\ \vdots & \vdots & \vdots & \ddots & \vdots \\ a_{i1} & a_{i2} & a_{i3} & \cdots & a_{in} \\ \vdots & \vdots & \vdots & \ddots & \vdots \\ a_{n1} & a_{n2} & a_{n3} & \cdots & a_{nn} \end{bmatrix} \cdot \begin{bmatrix} b_{11} & b_{12} & \cdots & b_{1j} & \cdots & b_{1n} \\ \vdots & \vdots & \ddots & \vdots & \ddots & \vdots \\ b_{i1} & b_{i2} & \cdots & b_{ij} & \cdots & b_{in} \\ \vdots & \vdots & \ddots & \vdots & \ddots & \vdots \\ b_{n1} & b_{n2} & \cdots & b_{nj} & \cdots & b_{nn} \end{bmatrix} =$$

Row i

$$= \begin{bmatrix} c_{11} & c_{12} & \cdots & c_{1j} & \cdots & c_{1n} \\ \vdots & \vdots & \ddots & \vdots & \ddots & \vdots \\ c_{i1} & c_{i2} & \cdots & c_{ij} & \cdots & c_{in} \\ \vdots & \vdots & \ddots & \vdots & \ddots & \vdots \\ c_{n1} & c_{n2} & \cdots & c_{nj} & \cdots & c_{nn} \end{bmatrix}$$

Entry on row i column j

Figure 1.20 Matrix multiple algorithm.

access a noncached memory location, and the CPU must access next, slower level of memory hierarchy
- Cache line size: this is defined as the number of bytes loaded together in one entry in the cache. This is usually a few machine words per entry
- Capacity: this is the amount of data that can be simultaneously stored in cache at any one time
- Associativity; the way in which cache is designed and used. A "direct-mapped" cache has only one address (line) in a given range in cache. An "n-way cache" has n ≥ 2 lines where different addresses can be stored

Lets take the example of a matrix multiply. We will consider a "naïve" version of matrix multiple and a "cache" version. The "naïve" version is the simple, triply-nested implementation we are typically taught in school. The "cache" version is a more efficient implementation that takes the memory hierarchy into account. A typical matrix multiply is shown in Figure 1.20.

One consideration with matrix multiplication is that row-major versus column-major storage pattern is language dependent.

Languages like C and C++ use a row-major storage pattern for 2-dimensional matrices. In C/C++, the last index in a multidimensional array indexes contiguous memory locations. In other words, a[i][j] and a[i][j + 1] are adjacent in memory. See Figure 1.21.

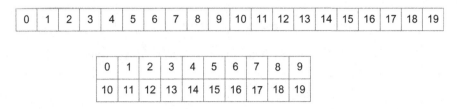

0	1	2	3	4	5	6	7	8	9	10	11	12	13	14	15	16	17	18	19

0	1	2	3	4	5	6	7	8	9
10	11	12	13	14	15	16	17	18	19

Figure 1.21 Row major storage ordering for C/C++.

Access by rows

```
for (i = 0; i < 5; i++)
        for (j = 0; j < 10; j++)
                a[i][j] = ...
```

Access by columns

```
for (j = 0; j < 10; j++)
        for (i = 0; i < 5; i++)
                a[i][j] = ...
```

Figure 1.22 Access by rows and by columns.

The stride between adjacent elements in the same row is 1. The stride between adjacent elements in the same column is the row length (10 in the example in Figure 1.21).

This is important because memory access patterns can have a noticeable impact on performance, especially on systems with a complicated multilevel memory hierarchy. The code segments in Figure 1.22 access the same elements of an array, but the order of accesses is different.

We can see this by looking at code for a "naïve" 512×512 matrix multiple shown in Appendix A. This code was run on a 4 core ARM-based multicore system shown in Figure 1.23.

The code to perform the matrix-matrix multiply is shown in Appendix A. Notice the structure of the triply-nested loop in the *_DoParallelMM* function: it's an *ijk* loop nest where the innermost loop (k) accesses a different row of B each iteration.

The code for a "cache friendly" matrix-matrix multiply is also in Appendix A. Interchange the two innermost loops, yielding an *ikj* loop nest. The innermost loop (j) should now access a *different* column of B during each iteration—along the same row. As we discussed above, this exhibits better cache behavior.

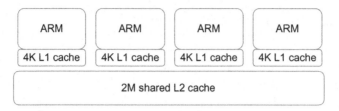

Figure 1.23 Four core ARM multicore system with private L1 and shared L2 cache.

We can apply additional optimizations, including "blocking." "Block" in this discussion does not mean "cache block." Instead, it means a subblock within the matrix we are using in this example.

As an example of a "block" we can break our matrix into blocks

$N = 8$; sub-block size $= 4$

$$\begin{bmatrix} A_{11} & A_{12} \\ A_{21} & A_{22} \end{bmatrix} \times \begin{bmatrix} B_{11} & B_{12} \\ B_{21} & B_{22} \end{bmatrix} = \begin{bmatrix} C_{11} & C_{12} \\ C_{21} & C_{22} \end{bmatrix}$$

Here is the way it works; Instead of the row access model that we just described;

```
/* row access method */
for (i = 0; i < N; i = i + 1)
  for (j = 0; j < N; j = j + 1)
    {r = 0;
    for (k = 0; k < N; k = k + 1){
        r = r + y[i][k]*z[k][j];};
    x[i][j] = r;
    };
```

With the blocking approach we use two Inner Loops. One loop reads all $N \times N$ elements of z[]. The other loop will read N elements of 1 row of y[] repeatedly. The final step is to write N elements of 1 row of x[].

Subblocks (i.e., A_{xy}) can be treated just like scalars in this example and we can compute;

$C_{11} = A_{11}B_{11} + A_{12}B_{21}$
$C_{12} = A_{11}B_{12} + A_{12}B_{22}$

$$C_{21} = A_{21}B_{11} + A_{22}B_{21}$$
$$C_{22} = A_{21}B_{12} + A_{22}B_{22}$$

Now a "blocked" matrix multiply can be implemented as;

```
for (jj = 0; jj < n; jj + = bsize) {
  for (i = 0; i < n; i++)
    for (j = jj; j < min(jj + bsize,n); j++)
      c[i][j] = 0.0;
  for (kk = 0; kk < n; kk + = bsize) {
    for (i = 0; i < n; i++) {
      for (j = jj; j < min(jj + bsize,n); j++) {
        sum = 0.0
        for (k = kk; k < min(kk + bsize,n); k++) {
          sum + = a[i][k] * b[k][j];
        }
        c[i][j] + = sum;
      }
    }
  }
}
```

In this example the loop ordering is bijk. The innermost loop pair multiplies a $1 \times$ bsize sliver of A by a bsize $\times$ bsize block of B and sums into $1 \times$ bsize sliver of C. We then loop over i steps through n row slivers of A & C, using the same B (See Figure 1.24).

Here is an excellent summary of cache optimizations (see page 6 in particular): http://www.cs.rochester.edu/~sandhya/csc252/lectures/lecture-memopt.pdf

The results are shown in Figure 1.25 part a. As you can see, row order access is faster than column order access.

Of course we can also increase the number of threads to achieve higher performance as shown in Figure 1.25 as well. Since this multicore processor has only has 4 cores, running with more than 4 threads—*when threads are compute-bound*—only causes the OS to "thrash" as it switches threads across the cores. At some point, you can expect the overhead of too many threads to hurt performance and slow an application down. See the discussion on Amdahl's Law!

The importance of caching for multicore performance cannot be overstated.

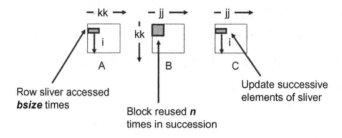

Figure 1.24 Blocking optimization for cache.

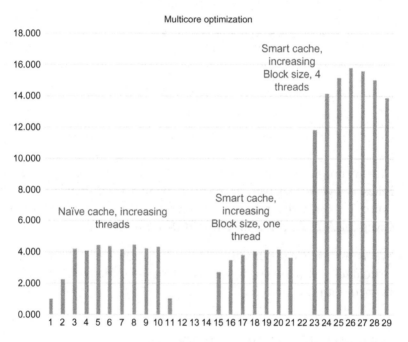

Figure 1.25 (a) Performance of naïve cache with matrix multiply (column order) and increasing threads, (b) row order and blocking optimizations with just one thread, and (c) row access with blocking caches and four threads of execution.

Remember back to my favorite "algorithm":

High-performance = parallelism + memory hierarchy − contention

You to need to not only expose parallelism, but you also need to take into account the memory hierarchy, and work hard to eliminate/minimize contention. This becomes increasingly true as the number of cores grows, and the speed of each core.

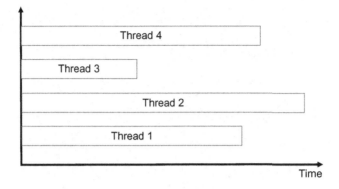

Figure 1.26 Load imbalance between threads on a multicore processor.

1.4.5 Load Imbalance

Load imbalance is the time that processors in the system are idle due to (Figure 1.26):

- insufficient parallelism (during that phase)
- unequal size tasks

Unequal size tasks can include things like tree-structured computations and other fundamentally unstructured problem. The algorithm needs to balance load where possible and the developer should profile the application on the multicore processor to look for load balancing issues. Resources can sit idle when load balancing issues are present (Figure 1.27)

1.4.6 Speedup

"Speedup" is essentially the measure of how much faster a computation executes versus the best serial code, or algorithmically:

Serial time/parallel time

As an example, suppose I am starting a car wash. I estimate it takes 20 min to wash a car. It also takes 10 min to set up the equipment to wash the car, and 15 min to break it down and put the equipment away. I estimate I will wash 150 cars in a weekend. If I hire one person to wash all of the cars, how long will this take? What if I hire 5 people that can all wash cars in parallel? How about 10 in parallel? Figure 1.28 shows the resulting speedup and efficiency improvements.

		Core1	Core2	Core3	Core4
Game	Bioshock	35%	25%	27%	11%
	Call of Duty 4	37%	27%	26%	10%
	Crysis	39%	44%	14%	2%
Image editing	Maya3D	41%	21%	5%	13%
	Photoshop	59%	17%	6%	10%
	Adobe Reader	36%	19%	5%	1%
Productivity	Excel	40%	12%	2%	0%
	PowerPoint	42%	16%	4%	1%
	Streets & Trips	34%	20%	5%	2%
Playback	iTunes 9	45%	24%	6%	1%
	QuickTime 7	39%	28%	23%	6%
	QuickTime HD	26%	22%	22%	19%
Video editing	Handbrake .9	88%	2%	10%	0%
	Powerdrive v8	58%	19%	11%	8%
Browsing	Firefox 3.5	42%	19%	9%	5%
	Safari 4.0	35%	21%	12%	8%

% Utilization of 1.6 GHz Quad
Processor*

Figure 1.27 Example load balancing for several applications. Source: Geoffrey Blake, Ronald G. Dreslinski, and Trevor Mudger, University of Michigan.

Efficiency can be defined as the measure of how effectively the computation resources (e.g., threads) are kept busy, or algorithmically:

Speedup/number of threads

Usually this is expressed as the average percentage of nonidle time

Efficiency is important because it is a measure of how busy the threads are during parallel computations. Low efficiency numbers may prompt the user to run the application on fewer threads/processors and free up resources to run something else (another threaded process, other user's codes).

The degree of concurrency of a task graph is the number of tasks that can be executed in parallel. This may vary over the execution, so we can talk about the *maximum* or *average*. The degree of concurrency increases as the decomposition becomes finer in granularity.

Number of car washers	Time	Speedup	Efficiency
1	10+15+(150*20) = 3025	1.0X	100%
5	10+15+(30*20) = 625	4.84X	96.8%
10	10+15+(15*20) = 325	9.3X	93%

Figure 1.28 Speedup and efficiency.

1.4.7 Directed Graphs

A *directed path* in a task graph represents a sequence of tasks that must be processed one after the other. The *critical path* is the longest such path. These graphs are normally weighted by the cost of each task (node), and the path lengths are the sum of weights.

We say that an instruction x precedes an instruction y, sometimes denoted $x < y$, if x must complete before y can begin.

In a diagram for the dag, $x < y$ means that there is a positive-length path from x to y.

If neither $x < y$ nor $y < x$, we say the instructions are in parallel, denoted x|y.

In Figure 1.29, we have, for example, $1 < 2$, $3 < 10$, and 4|22.

When we analyze a DAG as shown in Figure 1.29 we can estimate the total amount of "work" performed at each node (or instruction). "Work" is the total amount of time spent in all the instructions in Figure 1.29.

$$\text{Work Law:} Tp \geq T1/P$$

where

Tp: the fastest possible execution time of the application on P processors
T1: execution time on one processor

The "Span" of a DAG is essentially the "critical path" or the longest path through the DAG. Similarly, for P processors, the execution time is never less than the execution time on an infinite number of processors. Therefore, the Span Law can be stated as:

$$\text{Span Law:} Tp \geq T\infty$$

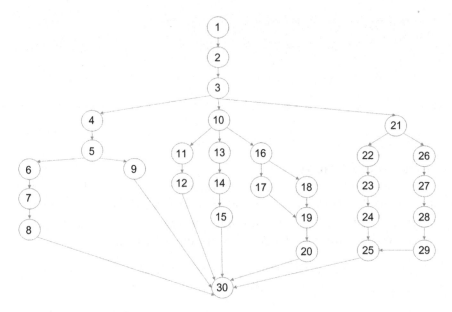

Figure 1.29 A directed asyclic graph (DAG).

Lets look at a quick example of how to compute "Work," "Span," and "Parallelism" but analyzing the DAG in Figure 1.29.

T(P) is the execution time of the program on P processors.
T(1) is the Work
T(∞) is the Span
Parallelism = T(1)/T(∞)
Work:
    T(1) = 30
Span:
    T(∞) = 10
which corresponds to the path $1 > 2 > 3 > 22 > 27 > 28 > 29 > 30 > 26 > 31$
Parallelism:
    T(1)/T(∞) = 30/10 = 3.0

See the excellent discussion by Charles Leiserson on this topic; http://www.akira.ruc.dk/~keld/teaching/IPDC_f10/How_to_Survive_the_Multicore_Software_Revolution-1.pdf.

CHAPTER 2

Parallelism in All of Its Forms

There are many forms of parallelism. We have been moving in this direction for many years, and they take different forms. Some of the key movements toward parallelism include:

- Bit-level parallelism
- Instruction-level parallelism (ILP)
- Simultaneous multithreading
- Single instruction, multiple data (SIMD)
- Data parallelism
- Task parallelism
- Accelerators/coprocessors

2.1 BIT-LEVEL PARALLELISM

We all know about this. Bit-level parallelism extends the hardware architecture to operate simultaneously on larger data. For example, on an 8-bit core, performing computation on a 16-bit data object requires two instructions. If we extend the word length (the native data length that a core works with) from 8 to 16, the operation can now be executed by a single instruction. You've seen this happen. As the computer industry has matured, word length has doubled from 4-bit cores through 8-, 16-, 32-, and 64-bit cores.

2.2 INSTRUCTION-LEVEL PARALLELISM (ILP)

Instruction-level parallelism (ILP) is a technique for identifying instructions that do not depend on each other, such as working with different variables and executing them at the same time (Figure 2.1). Because programs are typically sequential in structure, this takes effort which is why ILP is commonly implemented in the compiler or in superscalar hardware.

Multicore Software Development Techniques. DOI: http://dx.doi.org/10.1016/B978-0-12-800958-1.00002-4

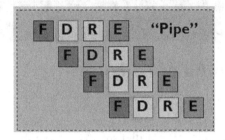

Figure 2.1 Processor pipeline.

Certain applications, such as signal processing for voice and video, can function efficiently in this manner. Other techniques in this area are speculative and out-of-order execution.

2.3 SIMULTANEOUS MULTITHREADING

With simultaneous multithreading (SMT), instructions from multiple threads are issued on same cycle. This approach uses register renaming and dynamic scheduling facilities of multi-issue architecture in the core. So this approach needs more hardware support, such as additional register files, program counters for each thread, and temporary result registers used before commits are performed. There also needs to be hardware support to sort out which threads get results from which instructions. The advantage of this approach is that it maximizes the utilization of the processor execution units. Figure 2.2 shows the distinction between how a superscalar processor architecture utilizes thread execution, versus a multiprocessor approach and the hyperthreading (or SMT) approach.

2.4 SINGLE INSTRUCTION, MULTIPLE DATA (SIMD)

Single instruction, multiple data (SIMD) is one of the architectures of Flynn's taxomony shown in Figure 2.3. This approach has been around for a long time. Since many multimedia operations apply the same set of instructions to multiple narrow data elements, having a computer with multiple processing elements that are able to perform the same operation on multiple data points simultaneously is an advantage.

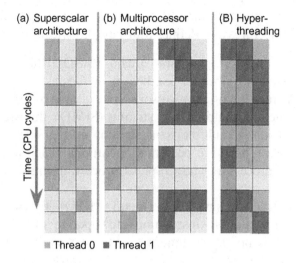

Figure 2.2 SMT requires hardware support but allows for multiple threads of execution per core.

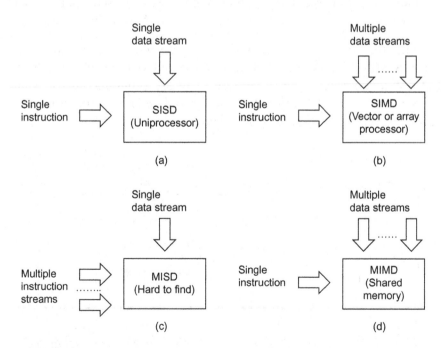

Figure 2.3 Flynn's taxonomy.

(Michael) Flynn's taxonomy is a classification system used for computer architectures and defines four key classifications.

- Single instruction, single data stream (SISD); this is sequential computer with no inherent parallelism in the instruction and data streams. A traditional uniprocessor is an example of SISD.
- Single instruction, multiple data streams (SIMD); this architecture is designed to allow multiple data streams and a single instruction stream. This architecture performs operations which are parallelizable. Array processors and graphics processing units fall into this category.
- Multiple instruction, single data stream (MISD); This architecture is designed allowmultiple instructions to operate on a single data stream. This is not too common today but some systems that are designed for fault tolerance may use this approach (like redundant systems on the space shuttle).
- Multiple instruction, multiple data streams (MIMD); in this approach multiple autonomous or independent processors simultaneously execute different instructions on different data. The multicore superscalar processors we discussed earlier are examples of MIMD architectures.

With that in mind lets discuss one of the more popular architectures, SIMD. This type of architecture exploits data level parallelism, but not concurrency. This is because there are simultaneous (or what we are calling parallel) computations, but only a single process (in this case, instruction) at a given cycle (Figure 2.4).

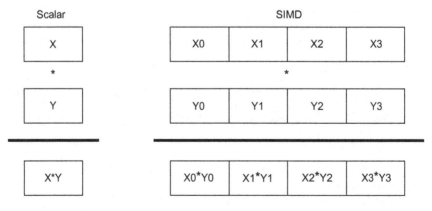

Figure 2.4 Scalar versus SIMD operations.

2.5 DATA PARALLELISM

Data parallelism is a parallelism approach where multiple units process data concurrently. Performance improvement depends on many cores being able to work on the data at the same time. When the algorithm is sequential in nature, difficulties arise. For example Crypto protocols, such as 3DES (triple data encryption standard) and AES (advanced encryption standard), are sequential in nature and therefore difficult to parallelize. Matrix operations are easier to parallelize because data is interlinked to a lesser degree (we have an example of this coming up).

In general, it is not possible to automate data parallelism in hardware or with a compiler because a reliable, robust algorithm is difficult to assemble to perform this in an automated way. The developer has to own part of this process.

Data parallelism represents any kind of parallelism that grows with the data set size. In this model, the more data you give to the algorithm, the more tasks you can have and operations on data may be the same or different. But the key to this approach is its scalability.

Figure 2.5 shows the scalable nature of data parallelism.

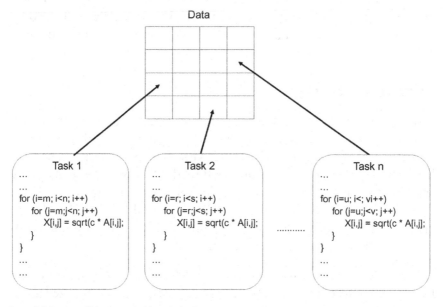

Figure 2.5 Data parallelism is scaleable with the data size.

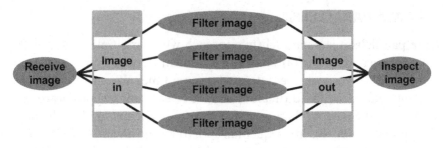

Figure 2.6 Data parallel approach.

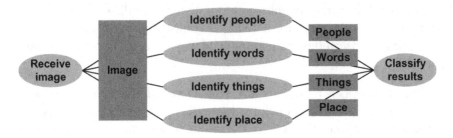

Figure 2.7 Task parallel approach.

In the example in Figure 2.6, an image is decomposed into sections or "chunks" and partitioned to multiple cores to process in parallel. The "image in" and "image out" management tasks are usually performed by one of the cores (an upcoming case study will go into this in more detail).

2.6 TASK PARALLELISM

Task parallelism distributes different applications, processes, or *threads* to different units. This can be done either manually or with the help of the operating system. The challenge with task parallelism is how to divide the application into multiple threads. For systems with many small units, such as a computer game, this can be straightforward. However, when there is only one heavy and well-integrated task, the partitioning process can be more difficult and often faces the same problems associated with data parallelism.

Figure 2.7 is an example of task parallelism. Instead of partitioning data to different cores, the same data is processed by each core (task), but each task is doing something different on the data.

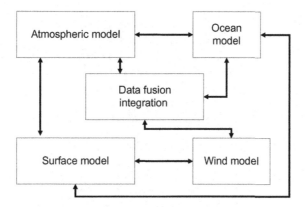

Figure 2.8 Function allocation in a multicore system (scalability limimted).

Task parallelism is about functional decomposition. The goal is to assign tasks to distinct functions in the program. This can only scale to a constant factor. Each functional task however can also be data parallel. Figure 2.8 shows this. Each of these functions (atmospheric, ocean, data fusion, surface, wind) can be allocated to a dedicated core but the scalability is only constant.

2.7 ACCELERATION AND OFFLOAD ENGINES

Many multicore processors also use hardware to assist in performing certain compute intensive operations. We call these "accelerators" or "offload engines." There are two types of accelerators:

- Data accelerators
- Algorithm accelerators

These accelerators often execute functions in parallel with other computation happening in the CPU, that is why we discuss them in this section.

Data accelerators move data independent of the CPU. The CPU sets up the transfer and then goes off to do other more useful things until the transfer of data is complete. DMA is most useful when the CPU cannot keep up with a high rate of data transfer or when the CPU needs to be utilized for more useful work while waiting for data to transfer.

Other data acclerators handle network traffic such as TCP/IP packets. These accelerators help mange and route data (packets) to different

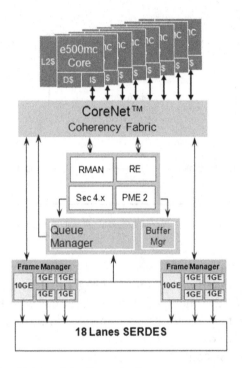

Figure 2.9 Multicore device with data and algorithm acceleration.

places in the multicore device. In Figure 2.9, the Frame Manager blocks and the Queue Manager and Buffer Manager are all considered data accelerators since they are used to manage and route data through the multicore device.

Algorithm accelerators perform specific algorithm operations with the use of dedicated hardware, and often times in parallel with the cores doing other work. Examples of these types of accelerators are:

• Cryptographic accelerator
• Pattern matching engine
• Video accelerator

In Figure 2.9 the Sec (Security Engine) is an algorithmic accelerator that does cryptography operations, and the PME (Pattern Matching Engine) performs this algorithm with the help of dedicated hardware.

As you can see, it is common for a multicore device to have both data accelerators and algorithmic accelerators.

CHAPTER 3

Multicore System Architectures

In this section we will discuss several types of multicore hardware architectures:

- Shared Memory Multicore Systems
- Distributed Memory Multicore Systems
- Hybrid Systems
- Symmetric and Asymmetric Multicore Systems

3.1 SHARED MEMORY MULTICORE SYSTEMS

In a shared memory multicore system, the individual processing units have local cache memories. There is also a shared memory between the processors (Figure 3.1). The key challenge in this approach is that the system must maintain a consistent view of shared memory between the processors. This is usually done in hardware and is called "cache coherence." More on this later.

In a shared memory system, multiple threads of execution are used to run multiple tasks simultaneously. Data shared between tasks running on each of the processors must be properly synchronized in the application (i.e., locks) in order to ensure dependency relationships are properly maintained. For example, in Figure 3.2, threads T1 and T2 may both need to read and write variable "A." Without synchronization, the order of reads and writes between the two threads is unpredictable, and three different outcomes are possible.

There are some key advantages of the shared memory approach. The key one is that globally shared memory provides a user-friendly programming perspective to application development.

Multicore Software Development Techniques. DOI: http://dx.doi.org/10.1016/B978-0-12-800958-1.00003-6

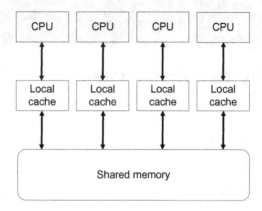

Figure 3.1 Shared memory multicore system.

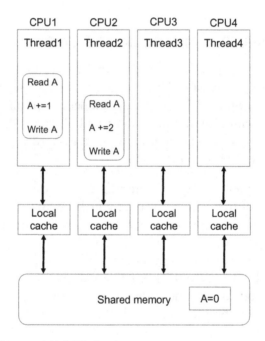

Figure 3.2 Race condition on variable "A" in shared memory.

The key downside or disadvantage to this approach is the lack of scalability (adding processors changes the traffic requirement of the Interconnect). Because of this is it is not so easy to build many core shared memory systems like this.

3.2 CACHE COHERENCY

Cache coherency is a situation where multiple processor cores share the same memory hierarchy, but have their own L1 data and instruction caches. Incorrect execution could occur if two or more copies of a given cache block exist, in two processors' caches, and one of these blocks is modified. Figure 3.2 shows the case where core 1 and core 2 both have a copy of variable "a" in their caches (steps 1 and 2). The variable was read from main memory (or an L2 cache) that both processors share, so both copies of the variable contain the same values. If core 1 or core 2 performs a read instruction to read a value in variable "a," correct execution occurs. However, if core 1 performs a store instruction (step 3) that modifies variable "a," and core 2 subsequently performs a load instruction from that variable, the read instruction must see the new value. Therefore, the new value must somehow be propagated to the copy of variable "a" in core 2. This is called the cache coherence problem (see Figure 3.3).

A set of rules that governs how multiple caches interact in order to solve this problem is called a cache coherence protocol.

One approach is to use what is called an invalidation-based cache coherence protocol. This approach solves the cache coherence problem by ensuring that as soon as a core requests to write to a cache block, that core must invalidate (remove) the copy of the block in any other core's cache that contains the block. The requesting core then has the only copy of the cache block, and can make modifications to its contents. Later, when any other core attempts to read the block, it will experience a cache miss, and must obtain the new data from the core that modified the data.

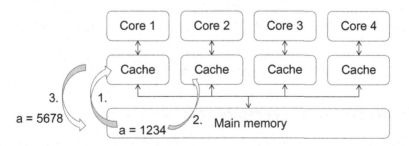

Figure 3.3 Cache coherence in a multicore system.

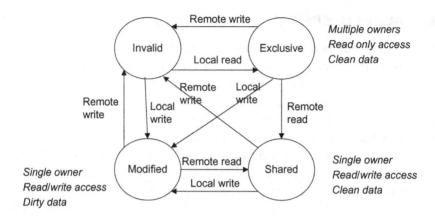

Figure 3.4 Basic MESI protocol state machine.

A common cache invalidation protocol is referred to as the MESI cache coherence protocol. This protocol is an invalidation-based protocol that is named after the four states that a cache block in an L1 cache can have:

- Modified: When a cache block is in this state, it is dirty with respect to the shared levels of the memory hierarchy. The core that owns the cache with the Modified data can make further changes at will.
- Exclusive: When a cache block is in this state, it is clean with respect to the shared levels of the memory hierarchy. If the owning core wants to write to the data, it can change the data state to Modified without consulting any other cores.
- Shared: When a cache data block is in this state, it is clean with respect to the shared levels of the memory hierarchy. The block is read-only. If a core wants to read a block in this Shared state, it may do so; however, if it wishes to write, then the block must be transitioned to the Exclusive state.
- Invalid: This state represents cache data that is not present in the cache.

The state machine is shown in Figure 3.4.

3.3 SHARED DATA SYNCHRONIZATION

Mutual exclusion using locks and semaphores is a common technique for ensuring that only one thread at a time may execute code with critical dependencies. In this approach, one thread holds a lock for a critical section. Other threads are now blocked from entering and using the shared data structure. In Figure 3.2, properly locking the critical section ensures that "A" always receives 3 as a final value.

Generally, each processor runs one thread at a time (ignore SMT for now). Additional threads may be created in the processor cores. When one thread blocks while waiting for the lock to clear, the operating system may wake up another ready thread to run in its place.

The cost of managing (acquiring and releasing) a lock can be significant. Locks, by definition, serialize code, so locking large critical sections will inhibit parallelism. Alternatively, using many, low-level locking primitives may lead to a large penalty for synchronization. The cost of creating and destroying completed tasks is also significant. The key lesson: the granularity of tasks and locking should match the available resources.

3.4 DISTRIBUTED MEMORY

Memory is not shared between systems in distributed memory systems. Each processor manages its own local memory (Figure 3.5). Communication of data between tasks running on different processors is accomplished by sending and receiving data between them using an approach called "message-passing." This is an example of difference programming models required for different multicore architectures;

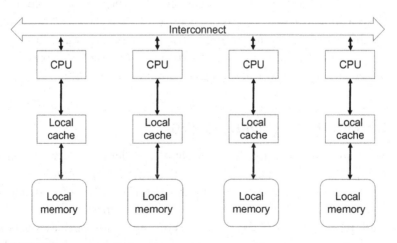

Figure 3.5 Distributed memory multicore system.

- Shared memory multicore systems; thread programming model
- Distributed or shared memory systems; message passing programming model

With the distributed memory model, data must be explicitly shared between tasks. Synchronization between tasks can be achieved by synchronous send-receive semantics. The receiving task blocks until the sending data is available. Message passing can also be asynchronous. With this approach, send-receive semantics are used and the receiving task checks or is notified when data is available without having to block. This allows the overlap of computation and communication which leads to noticeable performance gains. More on this later.

Relative to the shared memory, the distributed memory model usually leads to a higher overhead for communication (mainly in the setup and tear-down of a message and in explicit copying of data). Because of this, message passing should be optimized for both functions.

The other key advantages of the distributed model is the fact that memory is scalable with number of processors. So an increase in the number of processors and the size of memory increases proportionately. Another advantage is that each processor now has fast access to its own memory without interference from other cores, and without the overhead incurred with trying to maintain cache coherency. There is a cost advantage also. With this approach, it is more possible to use commodity, off-the-shelf processors, and networking.

The key disadvantage of this architecture is that the programmer is now responsible for the details associated with data communication. We will discuss some communication protocols that can make this easier. It may also be more difficult to map existing data structures, based on a global memory layout, to a distributed memory organization.

3.5 SYMMETRIC MULTIPROCESSING

Symmetric multiprocessing (SMP) systems are defined as two or more identical processors connected to a single, shared main memory. SMP systems have full access to all I/O devices (UART, communication controllers, etc.), and are controlled by a single operating system that views all processors equally, and reserves none for special purposes (Figure 3.6). Many multicore systems today are SMP systems. SMP

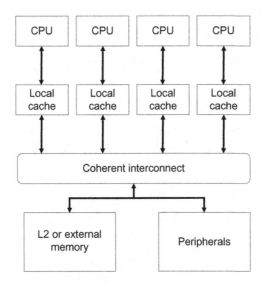

Figure 3.6 Symmetric multiprocessing (SMP) system.

systems are designed so that any processor can work on any task no matter where the data for that task is located in memory. Each task in the system should not be in execution on two or more processors at the same time.

Operating systems that support SMP systems can easily move tasks between processors to balance the workload as efficiently as possible. For example, to make use of SMP with Linux on SMP-capable hardware, the kernel must be properly configured. The CONFIG_SMP option must be enabled during kernel configuration to make the kernel SMP aware. The 2.6 Linux kernel version introduced a new O(1) scheduler that provides better support for SMP systems. The primary changes included the ability to load balance work across the available CPUs while maintaining some affinity for cache efficiency, since moving a task from one CPU to another, requires the cache to be flushed. This increases the latency of the task's memory access until the data is loaded into the cache of the new CPU.

Of course Linux (or any OS) support of SMP is not enough. The application developer must ensure that the application can be multi-threaded to exploit the power in SMP. We'll talk about this later.

An example of a SMP based system is shown in Figure 3.7. This multicore SoC has 12 physical cores and each core is dual threaded.

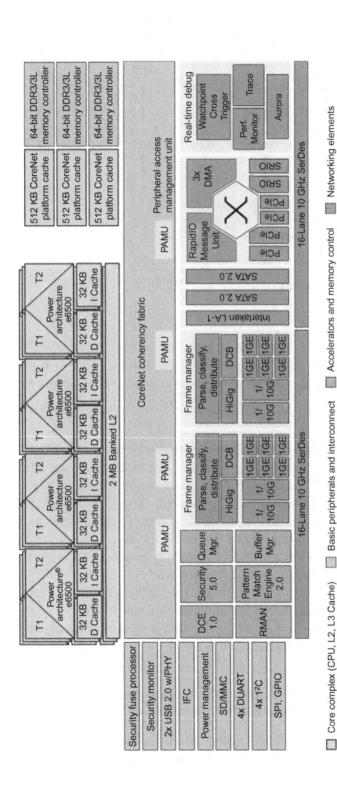

Figure 3.7 A homogeneous, multithreaded multicore device with data and algorithm acceleration.

Core complex (CPU, L2, L3 Cache)   Basic peripherals and interconnect   Accelerators and memory control   Networking elements

So from a software perspective, this is the equivalent of 24 cores. Each core is the same (an e6500 Power Architecture core) and Linux is the primary operating system. Linux has mechanisms to support SMP for this device. You can also see some of the data and algorithmic acceleration we spoke about earlier.

3.6 ASYMMETRIC MULTIPROCESSING

In an asymmetric multiprocessing system (AMP), all CPU's are not treated equally. First of all, the CPU's do not have to all be the same, they can be different core architectures and instruction sets. For example, in Figure 3.8, we have a general purpose CPU and a DSP core for presumably signal processing operations. AMP systems can also dedicate certain processors to focus on I/O operations with certain peripherals. This type of processor specialization may increase overall system performance.

AMP cores are more likely to have different operating systems and may or may not have shared memory. In Figure 3.8 Linux could run

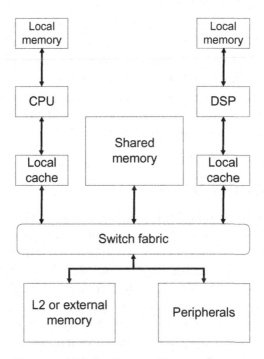

Figure 3.8 Asymmetric multiprocessor (AMP) system.

on the general purpose CPU and a RTOS can be configured to run on the DSP for real-time system applications. In AMP systems, tasks on different processors use messages for communications.

An example of a AMP system is shown in Figure 3.9. This AMP system has two general purpose (GPP) CPUs (Power Architecture e500 cores) and two DSP's (Starcore SC3850 cores). This is the type of device that would be used in an application that requires real-time signal processing and some control processing. The control processing would run on the GPPs and the signal processing would run on the DSPs. The GPP's run Linux and the DSPs run an RTOS as the operating system. You can see the shared memory in this system. Messages passing back and forth from the GPPs to the DSPs use this shared memory. You can also see an example of algorithmic acceleration in this device, the MAPLE baseband accelerator provides efficient processing for LTE applications that would run in a basestation application.

3.7 HYBRID APPROACHES

Of course SMP and AMP systems can be combined on to one multicore device as shown in Figure 3.10. This is a homogeneous multicore with 8 identical cores. Three of the cores are running Linux in an SMP configuration performing control based processing. The five remaining cores are running a RTOS and performing data processing on network packets. This system meets to requirement of AMP of having multiple operating systems and performing different tasks.

3.8 SPEAKING OF CORES

Lets talk about latency and throughput. What happens when you go to the doctor's office? You check in and wait for the doctor for your yearly checkup. The "latency" is the time you wait in the doctor's office for the doctor plus the time it takes for the doctor to give you your physical (Figure 3.11). The longer you wait, the worse your latency becomes. From the doctors perspective, she is primarily concerned with throughput, how many patients can she see per day. On a busy day she attempts to maximize throughput. Its better to have a nice long queue in the waiting room to help maximize throughput!

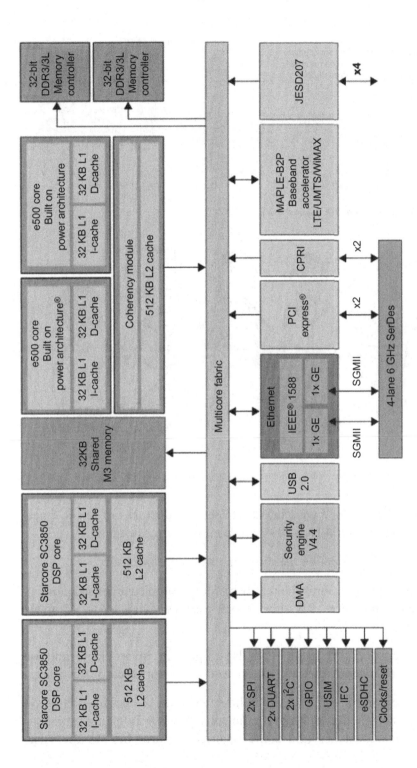

Figure 3.9 A heterogeneous multicore device (e500 GPP Cores and SC3850 DSP Cores) plus data and algorithm acceleration.

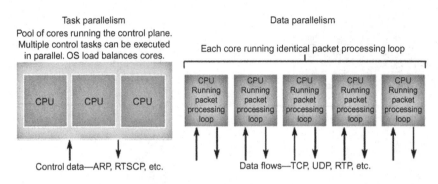

Figure 3.10 A hybrid SMP/AMP multicore system.

Figure 3.11 Latency and throughput as it relates to waiting for the doctor.

How can you reduce your latency to see the doctor? Go to the emergency room where latency, by definition, is shorter (usually).

So now we can define these two metrics more precisely:

- Throughput measures the number of jobs completed per second.
- Latency measures the time (worst-case or average) to complete a job.

Latency and throughput are also important to multicore and we need to understand when it is better to use one approach or the other.

Latency oriented CPUs are architected to make decisions based on situations (if-then-else) and to efficiently manage interrupts, branching, context switches and some security features besides the basic

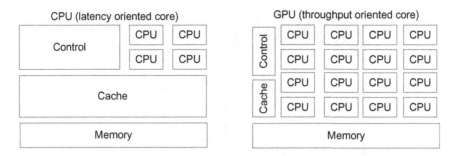

Figure 3.12 Latency and throughput oriented cores.

computation. CPU is much efficient in doing word processing application, management tasks, and other control oriented applications. But it is not efficient in processing many data streams simultaneously. This is where the GPU throughput oriented cores are better (Figure 3.12).

3.9 GRAPHICAL PROCESSING UNITS (GPU)

Graphical Processing Units (GPUs) are specialized devices whose sole purpose is to rapidly manipulate high volumes of graphical pixels. These devices were originally designed for use in advanced graphics and videogames. Today these multicore linear algebraic manipulations. But fundamentally GPUs are for massive data parallelism applications (Figure 3.12). GPUs use throughput oriented cores.

Many GPU applications will use a CPU and GPU together in a heterogeneous multicore environment. The sequential and control portions of the application run on the CPU and the computationally-intensive graphically oriented sections are accelerated by the GPU.

Another way to look at this partitioning is that the CPU focuses on doing complex manipulations on a small set of data, and the GPU focuses on performing simple manipulations to a large set of data.

3.10 PUTTING IT ALL TOGETHER

Of course, the choice does not have to be just one of these architectures. Many of the architectures we discussed above can be combined

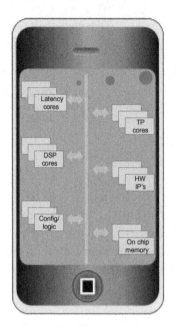

Figure 3.13 A heterogeneous multicore device where different cores are used for special purposes.

to get the right system design to support the application of choice. For example, a smart phone application can have a combination of:

- Latency oriented cores for user interface and control processing
- Throughput oriented cores for graphics processing
- Dedicated cores like DSPs for signal processing
- Acceleration (Hardware IP's) for efficient execution of certain algorithms like video processing

Figure 3.13 shows a configuration of a cell phone that utilizes all of these multicore processing elements. Of course with the cloud technology today, its also possible to offload processing to the cloud if necessary.

CHAPTER 4

Multicore Software Architectures

Software architectures for multicore are varied, depending on the application. But all architectures should take into consideration these concurrency factors:

- Decomposition; consider how the application can be decomposed into task and data parallelism
- Dependency analysis; consider both control and data dependences
- Design evaluation; look at the suitability for the target platform
- Design quality; consider what quality factors are important; performance, reliability, security, etc.

4.1 MULTICORE SOFTWARE ARCHITECTURES

4.1.1 Master/Worker
In this multicore architecture, one master thread executes code sequentially until it reaches an area that can be parallelized. The master then triggers a number of worker threads to perform the parallel computational intensive work. Once completed, the worker threads turn the result back to the master and wait for additional work. This is shown in Figure 4.1.

4.1.2 Peer
This software architecture is similar to the master/worker design with the master also functioning as a peer (worker) and shares the computational work. This approach can save a thread of execution (Figure 4.2).

Both master/worker and peer architectures are used for applications that have a sequential portion that is difficult to remove, which in turn requires a combination of concurrent and sequential execution.

Multicore Software Development Techniques. DOI: http://dx.doi.org/10.1016/B978-0-12-800958-1.00004-8

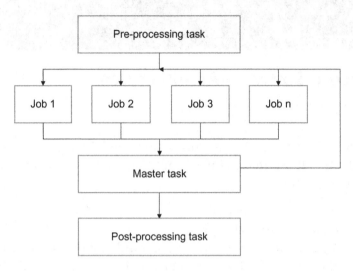

Figure 4.1 Master/worker multicore software architecture.

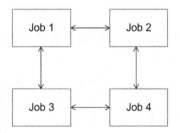

Figure 4.2 Peer to peer multicore software architecture.

4.1.3 Pipelined

A pipelined architecture involves dividing the applications into a series of smaller, independent stages. The output of one stage is the input to the next stage (Figure 4.3). Each one of the stages can be placed on a separate core. This forms a series of decoupled stages in the pipeline. These stages could be different protocol stack layers or specific functions such as encryption/decryption. Pipelined architectures can be very useful if the amount of parallelization is high. The key challenge is to balance the stages for constant throughput. The challenge is to tune the pipeline stages for similar execution latency so as to prevent any one stage from being a bottleneck for the rest of the system.

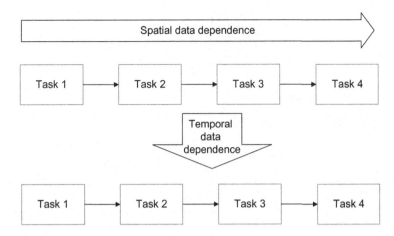

Figure 4.3 Pipelined multicore software architecture.

4.2 A DECISION TREE APPROACH TO SELECTING A MULTICORE ARCHITECTURE

The first step is being able to select the right multicore software architecture for the application. There are several ways to benefit from multicore processing. Software migrations will most likely start from serial code bases. Therefore, the target software design needs to identify the solution to meet the migration requirements.

There are several factors that will guide the plan for multicore migration. Factors include the starting point (design) of the original source code, as well as migration goals and constraints. Each method has its own strengths.

This section will walk through a multicore "decision tree" to select that multicore software architecture best suited to the application space under consideration. This decision tree is shown in Figure 4.4.

4.2.1 Decision 1: Select the Programming Model

The first decision is to decide whether the programming model should be symmetric multiprocessing (SMP) or asymmetric multiprocessing (AMP), keeping in mind that the application can be partitioned to support both.

Choose SMP if one operating system will be run, using all of the cores as equal processing resources, and the applications can be parallelized to benefit from SMP systems. SMP requires application analysis to

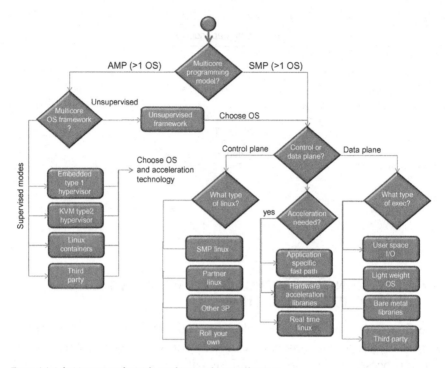

Figure 4.4 A decision tree used to pick a multicore software architecture.

identify opportunities for parallelism in the code and then rewriting the code to achieve this parallelism using multithreading. For CPU intensive code, which is difficult to redesign for parallel processing using SMP and multithreading, AMP could be a good alternative solution.

AMP requires no application changes to leverage the benefits of multiple cores. AMP leverages multiple cores by running multiple instances of the OS and application in separate partitions that are dedicated to specific cores, peripherals, and system memory areas. This can be beneficial when an increased level of security is required on some cores. Devices are assigned to cores and the I/O connections and secure applications are separated by the MMU.

Keep in mind, AMP requires a boot loader that supports AMP and to partition the hardware resources and make OS and application assignments to those partitions. The OS must be relocatable, must be able to restrict its memory region, and must only operate on its assigned PCI devices.

4.2.2 Decision 2: Choose the Operating System Framework

If AMP is chosen, the next step is to determine which Multicore Operating System Framework is required.

Unsupervised AMP runs multiple operating systems on the cores. This has the advantage of being able to keep the system "up" if one of the OSs crashes. Establishing the separation of multiple OSs on top of a single processor with shared memory can be problematic. AMP partitioning can solve the scalability problem of SMP, but only if the algorithm is well parallelizable. This is usually a problem left for the system integrator.

If unsupervised AMP is not the right choice then there are a number of "supervised" AMP options as shown in Figure 1. There are three primary supervised AMP options using virtualization.

Virtualization provides a software management layer that provides software protection between the different partitions as well as core management in order to optimize power efficiency. The CPUs are run as multiple independent partitions running their own OS and application. For applications designed using multiple components that are independent and CPU bound with little contention to shared resources, this is the way to go.

Legacy software changes are not needed when using virtualization to partition multiple OSs to run within virtual machines (VMs). The Virtual Machine Manager (VMM) manages the assignment and access between the VMs and platform resources.

A number of software technologies are available to enable virtualization in embedded systems;

- OS-level virtualization; uses the capabilities of an operating system kernel to enable multiple isolated instances of user-space. Each user space instance has its own private, isolated set of standard operating system resources, and applications run in this isolated "container." Linux containers are an example of OS-level virtualization. Containers are used in situations that require application consolidation, sandboxing, or dynamic resource management and all the software domains involved are Linux applications. It is not possible to boot an operating system in a container.

- "Type 1" hypervisors; a "type 1" hypervisor runs directly on system hardware, and is not part of a general purpose operating system. These are generally small, efficient hypervisors that enable the secure partitioning of a system's resources. A system's CPUs, memory, and I/O devices are statically partitioned, with each partition being capable of running a guest operating system. Hypervisors do not use schedulers and simply spatially partition the CPUs.
- "Type 2" hypervisors; type 2 hypervisors use an operating system as the basis for the virtualization layer. Virtual machines run alongside other OS applications. An example of a type 2 hypervisor is KVM (kernel-based virtual machine). KVM is an open source software virtualization technology also based on the Linux kernel. KVM enables Linux to act as a virtual machine monitor. KVM is essentially a Linux kernel driver that collaborates with a QEMU user space application to create and run virtual machines.

Virtualization and partitioning in embedded systems enable some benefit to be gained from multi-core processors independent of explicit OS support. The ideal situation is to have symmetric multiprocessing and asymmetric multiprocessing, including virtualization, at your disposal.

A summary of these primary multicore software configurations is shown in Figure 4.5.

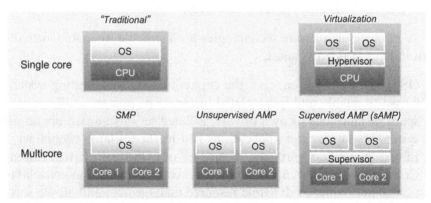

Arbitrary combinations of these primary configurations can be used to create more advanced configurations.

Figure 4.5 Primary multicore software configurations.

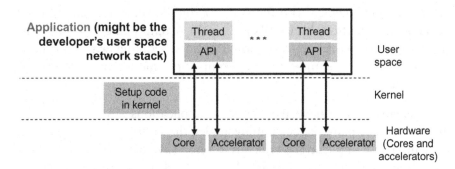

Figure 4.6 User space applications and I/O.

4.2.3 Decision 3: Determine the Control Plane and Data Plane Model

If we go down the SMP side of the decision tree we must choose whether our SMP configuration will be "data plane" or "control plane" focused. Data plane configurations are throughput intensive (e.g., packets per second) and usually need a lightweight or real-time operating system, or another lightweight programming model for handling throughput requirements on the data plane side.

For performance sensitive applications where throughput is important, one such approach that is gaining popularity in the multicore space is "user space" application development. It is a framework of Linux user space drivers that allow customers to develop high-performance solutions (Figure 4.6). Its high-performance stems from doing I/O that bypasses the Linux kernel so no system calls are needed. Application developers with their own software often like this model. Another advantage is keeping application software out of the kernel to avoid GPL license contamination.

4.2.4 Decisions 4 and 5: Choose the Type of Operating System Needed for the Control Plane and Data Plane

Data plane processing, in many cases, does not require an operating system. There is typically no requirement or need to provide services to a user or otherwise restrict access to the underlying hardware through a restrictive set of APIs. In addition, fast path processing does not require direct intervention by the user as packet processing is done automatically. Many of the other functions are typically handled by an OS, such as process management (there is usually only one task per core), memory management (pre-allocated buffers are used), file management (no file system), and device management (low level access functions and APIs are used). A data plane OS is used to support legacy code or to do some basic scheduling when the need arises. Choose a simple run to completion model or a RTOS if necessary.

It is common to have the multicore applications that are allocated to the control plane layer running under the control of an operating system. These applications typically do not have any real-time latency or throughput constraints as it relates to packet processing. Much of the complex processing required on the control plane and the need to reuse existing code bases makes the interaction with an OS a prerequisite. Linux is a common choice for an operating system for control plane processing as it has added increased support for SMP processing. Some of the improvements include an adjustment to the way the kernel supports the file systems, a number of routing and device-handling optimizations, removal of the Big Kernel Lock (BKL) which should increase Linux performance on larger SMP-based systems, the ability to throttle input and output, improved power management, and upgrades to the CPU scheduler.

4.2.5 Decision 6: Determine the Type of Acceleration Needed

Multicore network acceleration is necessary for packet processing. TCP/IP stacks are not designed to work well with multicore systems.

Most network packet processing protocols can be broken down into two paths;

- Stateless path, also known as the data path, requires quick and efficient switching/routing of packets. This can be broken down into packet identification (classification) and forwarding.
- Stateful path, also known as the control path, requires more processing and has more inherent latency than the data path.

The stateful control path requires 90% of the code and is used 10% of the time. The stateless data path requires just 10% of the code and is used 90% of the time (Figure 4.7).

Fast Path technology is used to accelerate the 10% of the code in the stateless path to increase packet processing performance.

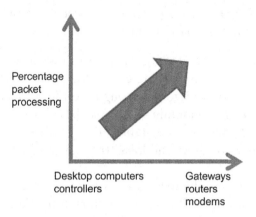

Figure 4.7 System CPU cycle allocation.

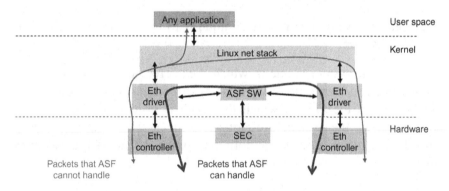

Figure 4.8 Application specific fast path.

Application Specific Fast Path (ASF) is a software-based solution that stores flows requiring simple, deterministic processing in a cache. ASF recognizes cached flows and processes such packets in a separate highly optimized context (Figure 4.8).

ASF accelerates the data throughput for networking devices. ASF in software provides optimized implementation for Data Path processing that is customized for platforms for achieving higher throughput for specific applications. It leverages functionality provided by hardware like hashing, checksum calculation, cryptography, classification, scheduling to provide higher throughput.

The focus of ASF is to accelerate the processing of many relevant applications. Some examples include:

- IPv4 Forwarding—Create an ASF forwarding cache. When packets match entries in the forwarding cache, the packets get forwarded at the driver level, without going through the Linux Networking Stack.
- Firewall + NAT—Maintain a 5 tuple based session table. When packets match the session table, the packets can be scanned for vulnerabilities, have address translation performed and be forwarded.
- IPsec—Maintain a database of associations from flows to SA (Security Association). When packets match the database, the packets are encrypted or decrypted and routed appropriately.
- IP Termination—Accelerate the preconfigured locally terminated or originated flows. Can work in conjunction with PMAL-user-space Zero Copy Mechanism.

An alternative acceleration technique is to use Linux as a real-time operating system.

A real-time system is one in which the correctness of the computations depends not only upon the logical correctness of the computation but also upon the time at which the result is produced. If the timing constraints of the system are not met, the system will fail. Many embedded systems now have both real-time and nonreal-time tasks running on the OS (Figure 4.9).

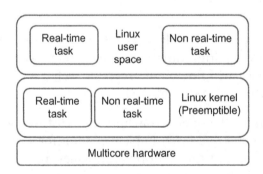

Figure 4.9 Linux supports real-time tasks with Real-Time extensions.

It is very difficult to design a system that provides both low latency and high performance. However, real-world systems (such as Media, eNodeB, etc.) have both latency and throughput requirements. For example, an eNodeB basestation has a 1 ms hard real-time processing deadline for Transmission Time Interval (TTI) as well as a throughput requirement of 100 Mbps downlink (DL) and 50 Mbps (UL). This requires the need to tune the system for the right balance of latency and performance.

Linux now provides soft real-time performance through a simple kernel configuration to make the kernel fully preemptable. In the standard Linux kernel, when a user space process makes a call into the kernel using a system call, it cannot be preempted. This means that if a low-priority process makes a system call, a high-priority process must wait until that call is complete before it can gain access to the CPU. The Linux configuration option CONFIG_PREEMPT changes this behavior of the kernel and allows Linux processes to be preempted if high-priority work is available, even if the process is in the middle of a system call.

RT-Linux also makes the system preemptive including more granular spin-locks, making the interrupt handlers kernel threads by default, and allowing higher priority tasks even if in user-space to preempt lower priority tasks at any point of time.

After working your our way through the multicore decision tree, we end up at a set of leaf nodes that describe the reference software architecture needed to implement the high level system software requirements (path through the decision tree) for the multicore system. Some of these examples are shown in Figure 4.10.

We've discussed a number of multicore software architecture components as we assemble our multicore reference architectures. In fact we can view these architectural components as a set of building blocks or Lego bricks that can be put together in different ways to create the multicore software reference architecture (Figure 4.11). This approach can produce a scalable solution customized to the needs of the developer for a variety of multicore software solutions.

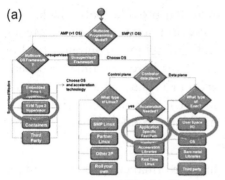

Example 1:
Open source virtualization (KVM)
with linux OS and user space I/O
and application specific
fast path multicore software
reference architecture

ASF = Application specific fast path

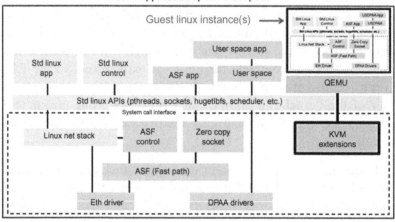

Figure 4.10 (a) Multicore software reference architecture requiring an open source virtualization solution (KVM), a Linux OS on the control plane with high performance user space I/O requirements and a fast path capability for required data flows; (b) Multicore software reference architecture requiring an light weight embedded virtualization solution, two Linux OS partitions on the control plane with high performance user space I/O requirements and a fast path capability for required data flows; (c) Multicore software reference architecture requiring a Linux SMP solution on the control plane with a lightweight data plane environment and a fast path capability for required data flows.

(b)

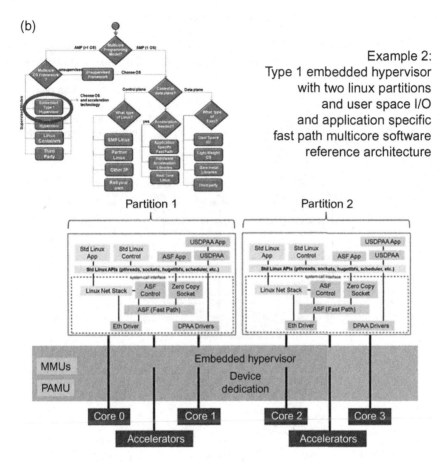

Example 2:
Type 1 embedded hypervisor
with two linux partitions
and user space I/O
and application specific
fast path multicore software
reference architecture

Figure 4.10 (Continued).

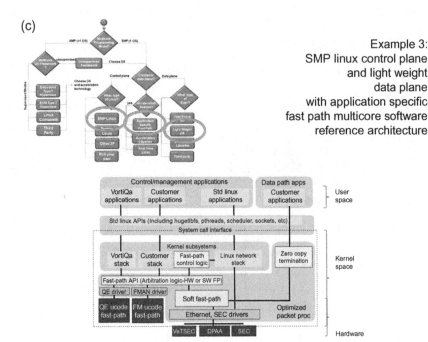

(c)

Example 3:
SMP linux control plane
and light weight
data plane
with application specific
fast path multicore software
reference architecture

Figure 4.10 (Continued).

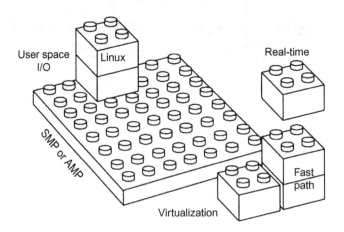

Figure 4.11 Multicore software architecture is solution-based on collaborating components.

CHAPTER 5

Multicore Software Development Process

Multicore development follows these basic steps;

1. Define the work to be done
2. Manually determine concurrency
3. Add some additional data required to make concurrency easier
4. Organize into an algorithm
5. Determine the partitioning
6. Determine the communication model
7. Map the processing to the multicore processor

We can show this graphically in Figure 5.1. Shortly we will introduce a case study to show how this works.

5.1 MULTICORE PROGRAMMING MODELS

A "Programming Model" defines the languages and libraries that create an abstract view of a machine. For multicore programming, the programming model should consider the following;

- Control. Control defines how parallelism is created and how dependencies (orderings) are enforced. An example of this would be to define the explicit number of threads of execution.
- Data. This defines how and whether data can be shared or whether it will be all private. For shared data, this also defines whether that data is shared data accessed or private data communicated. For example, what is the access to global data from multiple threads? What is the control of the data distribution to execution threads?
- Synchronization. This part of the programming model defines what operations can be used to coordinate parallelism and what are the atomic (indivisible) operations. An example of this is communication, and what data transfer parts of the language will be used or what libraries are used. Another example would be to define explicitly the mechanisms to regulate access to data. Figure 5.2 is an

Multicore Software Development Techniques. DOI: http://dx.doi.org/10.1016/B978-0-12-800958-1.00005-X

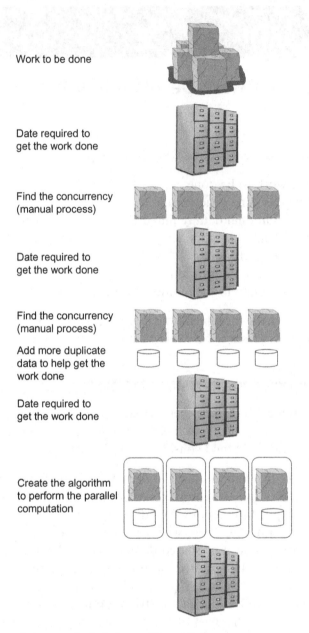

Work to be done

Date required to
get the work done

Find the concurrency
(manual process)

Date required to
get the work done

Find the concurrency
(manual process)

Add more duplicate
data to help get the
work done

Date required to
get the work done

Create the algorithm
to perform the parallel
computation

Figure 5.1 Key steps in the process for developing a multicore application.

example of a programming model decision between threading
(shared memory) and message passing. As we will see soon, this
drives decisions on which technology to use in multicore
development.

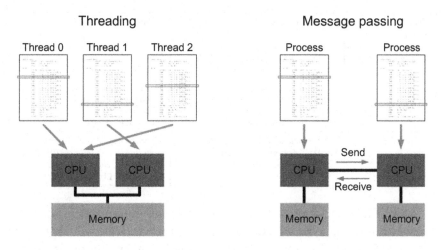

Figure 5.2 Multicore programming model decision (threading use of shared memory or message passing).

The shared memory paradigm in some ways is similar to sequence programming, but the developer must explicitly specify parallelism and use some mechanism (locks/semaphors) to control access to the shared memory. Sometimes this is called "directive-based" and we can use technologies like OpenMP to help us with this.

The choice is explicit from a parallel programming perspective. We can use threads which is common with shared memory system and focus on synchronization. Or we can use a technology like "Message Passing Interface" (MPI) which is based on message passing systems where the focus is on communication not so much synchronization.

Determining the right programming model for multicore is dependent on several factors;

- The type of multicore processor; different multicore processors support different types of parallelism and programming.
- The level of abstraction required, from "do it yourself" (DIY) multicore to using abstraction layers.

For example, below are some multicore processors types and how they are designed/optimized to support multicore. So when deciding on a programming model, be sure to understand whether or not the processor you want to use supports the programming model you are interested in (A good summary is described in http://www.sandia.gov/~ktpedre/papers/multicore-tech.pdf).

Multicore Processor Type	Parallelism Supported	Architectural Features
AMD quad core Opteon	SIMD, Task Level parallelism (TLP), memory level parallelism (MLP)	SIMD unit (SIMD), enhanced on chip memory controllers (MLP), memory and cache controllers (TLP)
Intel Xeon	Instruction level parallelism (ILP), SIMD, Task Level parallelism (TLP), memory level parallelism (MLP)	2 64-bit cores, dedicated L1, common L2 optimized for data sharing, optimized memory controller
Freescale T4240	Instruction level parallelism (ILP), SIMD, Core Level parallelism (CLP), memory level parallelism (MLP)	Altivec engine (SIMD), 12 e6500 multi-threaded 64 bit cores (24 virtual cores) (CLP), clustered L2 cache controller (MLP), multi-issue (ILP)

Also, when deciding on a multicore programming model, take into consideration the type of computation required. This will determine what programming model to choose and what other support is needed (operating system, etc.). Here are some examples below;

Type of Programming Required	Choose a Processor that Supports these Types of Parallelism	Other Support Required
Vector instructions	Memory level parallelism, SIMD	None
Implicit threading	Task level parallelism (TLP), Core level Parallelism (CLP), Memory Level Parallelism (MLP)	Lightweight thread support or active threads; thread-safe libraries; libraries that use threading capabilities to achieve parallelism
Multi threading with compiler support (e.g., OpenMP)	Task level parallelism (TLP), Core level Parallelism (CLP), Memory Level Parallelism (MLP)	Shared memory capabilities within a process; POSIX thread support and/or compliance with compiler generated or OpenMP-generated function calls
Explicit message passing (e.g., MPI)	Core level Parallelism (CLP) and/ or Task level parallelism (TLP), Memory Level Parallelism (MLP)	Efficient network stack; matching capabilities for incoming messages; interprocess, intranode communication mechanisms

CHAPTER 6

Putting it All Together, A Case Study of Multicore Development

We've discussed a number of multicore concepts so far. Let's use a case study to show how some of these concepts would come together in a multicore application. We will discuss how to map a JPEG encoding algorithm on to a multicore processor and all of the challenges and opportunities that go along with that. Let's start by looking at Figure 6.1.

This processor is a homogeneous device and so we will attempt to develop a SMP application that takes advantage of this architecture. There are three areas that should always be considered when developing an application on an SMP device, described in Table 6.1.

There are two general multicore processing models applicable to an SMP device:

- Multiple-single-cores in which the cores in an SMP environment execute an application independent of each other.
- Cooperating-multiple-cores in which the cores in an SMP environment cooperate in some fashion to perform the application.

6.1 MULTIPLE-SINGLE-CORES

An example of "Multiple-Single-Cores" is shown in Figure 6.2.

In a multiple-single-cores software model, all cores in the system execute their application independently of each other. The applications running on each core can be identical or different. This model is the simplest way to port an application to a multicore environment, because the individual processors are not required to interact. Thus, porting basically involves replicating the single-core application on each of the corresponding cores on the multicore system.

Multicore Software Development Techniques. DOI: http://dx.doi.org/10.1016/B978-0-12-800958-1.00006-1

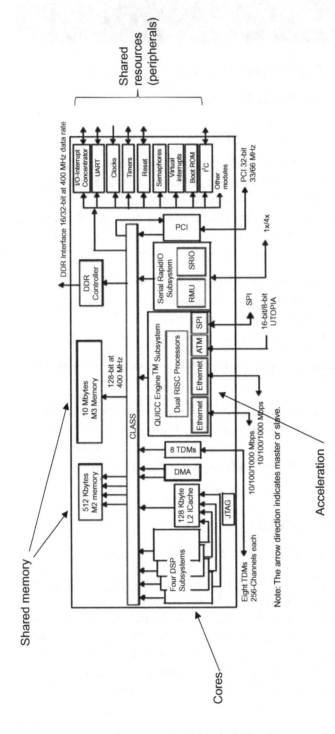

Figure 6.1 A four core multicore processor with data acceleration.

Table 6.1 Key Areas of Concern for a SMP Application	
Areas to Consider	Description
Scheduling	The scheduling methodology for an application allocates the resources in the multicore system, primarily by managing the processing of the cores to meet the timing and functional requirements of the application most effectively.
Intercore communications	The interaction between cores in a multicore environment is largely used for passing messages between cores and for sharing common system resources such as peripherals, buffers, and queues. In general, the OS includes services for message passing and resource sharing.
Input and output	The management of input and output data. Defines the partitioning and allocation of input data among the cores for processing and the gathering of output data after processing for transfer out of the device.

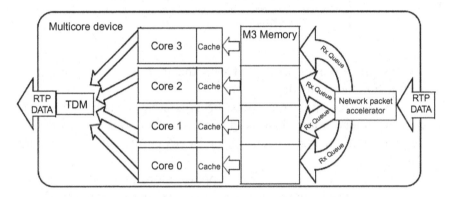

Figure 6.2 Multiple-single-cores model of SMP.

The developer replicates single-core application on each of the cores in the multicore system such that their processing does not interfere with each other. An example of this approach is a Media Gateway for a voice over IP (VoIP). Each core executes independently from the other cores in the DSP cores using data streams corresponding to distinct user channels.

One broad benefit of the multiple-single-cores model is that scaling the system by the addition of cores to the system, or by increasing the functional complexity of the application executing on each core can be as straightforward as making the same change on a single-core system, assuming other system constraints such as bus throughput, memory, and I/O can support the increased demand.

The multiple-single-cores model has the following characteristics;

- A single core in the multicore system is capable of meeting the requirements of the application using the corresponding portion of

Table 6.2 Summary of Advantages of "Multiple-Single-Cores" Model	
Areas to Consider	**Advantage**
Scheduling	The lack of intentional interaction between cores precludes the need for task scheduling and load balancing between cores. Consequently, the associated complexity and overhead is eliminated which results in a more predictable system that is easier to maintain and debug.
Intercore communications	Independent core operation eliminates the need for intercore communication and its resulting overhead. This also minimizes data coherency issues between cores.
Input and output	The cores are not involved in partitioning or distributing the input or output data. Although the input data for a device may arrive through a single peripheral device or DMA controller, the data is partitioned into independent "streams" for each core by the hardware peripheral. Thus no software intervention by the core is required to determine which portion of the incoming data belongs to it. The same applies to Output data. It can be reassembled into a single output stream by the peripheral hardware from the independent data streams coming from each core, and then be transmitted over the appropriate output port(s).

the system resources associated with that core (memory, bus bandwidth, IO, and so forth).

- The I/O for the application must be assignable to each core with no runtime intervention. The assignment of data to a core occurs at compile time, at system-startup, or by an entity outside the multicore device.
- The multiple-single-core model supports more predicable execution because the application executes on a single core without any dependence or interaction with other cores. Thus, applications that have a complicated control path or very strict real-time constraints are better suited to a multiple-single-cores implementation.
- The application has a data processing path consisting of tasks or functional modules that efficiently use the caches on the device. An application that has processing modules that do not use caches efficiently may require partitioning among multiple cores so the caches do not thrash.

The advantages and disadvantages of this approach are summarized in Tables 6.2 and 6.3.

6.2 COOPERATING-MULTIPLE-CORES

An example of "Cooperating-Multiple-Cores" is shown in Figure 6.3.

In the cooperating-multiple-cores model, the cores in a multicore environment cooperate with each other and thus better utilize the

Table 6.3 Summary of Disadvantages of "Multiple-Single-Cores" Model	
Areas to Consider	**Disadvantage**
Scheduling	Applications using the model may have cases in which some cores are overloaded while others are minimally loaded or even idle. This occurs simply because the system does not have a way of scheduling the processing tasks among the cores; each core must process the data assigned to it.
Intercore communications	Inability to communicate or dynamically assign tasks between cores.
Input and output	The I/O peripherals must be capable of partitioning the data into independent streams for each core. In the example shown in Figure 6.2, the MSC8144 QUICC Engine subsystem supports the multiple I/O ports necessary to interface to the IP network. In addition, the operating system or framework used to execute the application must provide adequate services to manage the I/O devices.

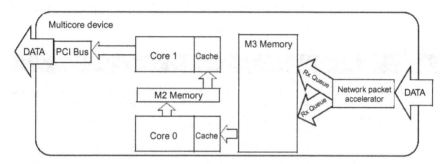

Figure 6.3 Cooperating-multiple-cores model of SMP.

system resources available for the application. For some applications, the cooperating-multiple-cores model is the only option because the application is too complex or large to process using the multiple-single-cores model. In a cooperating-multiple-core system the cores do not generally perform identical tasks because the processing is partitioned among the cores, either at the application level, the scheduling, the I/O or in some other manner.

In Figure 6.3, Core 0 and Core 1 each perform different portions of the application processing. The input stream is used by Core 0 and the output data is generated by Core 1. Intermediate results are passed between Core 0 and Core 1.

The advantages and disadvantages of the cooperating-multiple-cores model are summarized in Tables 6.4 and 6.5.

Table 6.4 Summary of Advantages of "Cooperating-Multiple-Cores" Model	
Area to Consider	Advantage
Scheduling	The scheduler for true-multiple-cores has the ability to dynamically manage the system resources as a whole. This scheduling can be implemented in different ways. The scheduling intelligence can be centralized in a single core which assigns tasks to the remaining cores in the system, or distributed among multiple cores in the system with each core deciding which tasks to perform. In either situation, the system resources are better utilized and thus the performance of the application is maximized.
Intercore communications	The nature of this communication is application specific and generally involves the passing of control and status information between the cores. The messages can be to a specific core or broadcast to all the cores. In general, the OS provides the necessary mechanisms for the intercore communications through an API. The communication between cores allows the cores to cooperate with each other.
Input and out	In true-multiple-cores. It is possible to have a centralized entity, such as a core, manage the I/O for the application. This has the advantage that it can reduce the overall overhead associated with managing the I/O.

Table 6.5 Summary of Disadvantages of "Cooperating-Multiple-Cores" Model	
Areas to Consider	Disadvantage
Scheduling	The scheduler incurs overhead in the system, which can adversely affect the real-time requirements of the application. This must be offset by the increase in performance obtained from the cores cooperating with each other.
Intercore communications	The overhead due to messages going between the cores can also negatively affect the performance of the application. Furthermore, the dependencies between tasks executing in different cores will also affect the performance of the system as a whole.

6.3 GETTING STARTED

The first major activity in porting an application from a single to multicore environment is to identify the threads or tasks that can execute concurrently by the multiple cores. Use the following general guidelines when determining and evaluating these tasks:

- Choose tasks with real-time characteristics. The tasks in a multicore environment should have clearly defined real-time characteristics just as they do in a single core application.
- Avoid tasks that are too short. The overhead associated with short tasks is proportionally more significant than for larger tasks. Overpartitioning an application with the aim of providing flexibility and concurrency will generally create a large number of tasks and priorities spread out over several cores complicating the scheduler, increasing overhead, and making it harder to implement and debug.

- Minimize the dependencies between cores. Overdesigning the tasks and their interaction complicates the application and makes the system more difficult to implement and debug. Intercore dependencies also incur an overhead.
- Task execution in a single core device forces tasks to execute sequentially. In a multicore environment, the same tasks can execute concurrently and tasks do not necessarily complete in the same order as in a single core. A multicore environment can expose dependencies that are hidden in a single core environment. Consider a simple application with three tasks A, B, and C that execute at the same priority. Task C can execute only after tasks A and B have completed. In a single core environment the application can be written such that task A triggers B which then triggers C. In a multicore device, tasks A and B can execute simultaneously on separate cores, so task C must now wait for both tasks A and B to begin execution, not just task B as in the single core environment. Though this is a simple example, consider a more realistic situation in which several cores execute many prioritized tasks whose execution time may change at runtime due to dependencies on the data being processed.

6.3.1 JPEG Encoding Application

A motion JPEG application is to be ported to a multicore processor using the methods discussed above.

A summary of this application is shown in Figure 6.4. The input data stream consists of a real-time sequence of raw video images (frames) that arrive over the network connection.

The multiple cores all cooperate in the processing of the video stream by encoding a portion of the current frame using the JPEG compression algorithm. The output data stream is then reassembled into the same order in which it was received and it is sent back over the network connection in this encoded format to a personal computer (PC) where it is decoded (uncompressed) and displayed real-time.

The input video stream consists of continuous raw digital images partitioned into blocks of pixels called Minimum Coded Units (MCUs). An MCU consists of a 16×16 array of 8-bit pixels composed of 256 bytes of luminance information (Y) and 256 bytes of chrominance (Cb and Cr) information. Luminance is provided for every pixel in the image and chrominance is provided as a medium

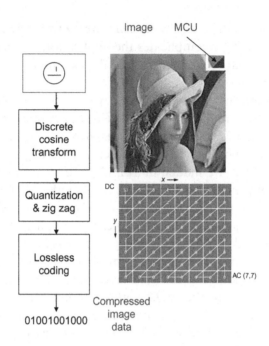

Figure 6.4 JPEG encoding algorithm.

value for a 2×2 block of pixels. The 512-byte MCU is partitioned into four 8×8 pixels blocks that serve as inputs to the Discrete Cosine Transfer (DCT) processing block. There is no relation between any two MCU blocks.

The purpose of the DCT is to convert the information in the original raw pixels blocks into a spatial frequency representation of the block. These spatial frequencies represent the level of detail in the image. Thus, a block with a lot of detail in it has many high spatial frequency components while blocks with low detail are represented by a majority of low frequency components. Typically, most of the information is concentrated in a few low-frequency components. The DCT is applied to an 8×8 block of pixels from left to right and from top to bottom of an image frame.

The result is a new 8×8 block of integers (called DCT coefficients) that are then reordered using a zig-zag pattern. The 8×8 block of DCT coefficients is traversed using a zig-zag pattern. The result of this reordering is a vector of 64 elements (0 to 63) arranged from lowest to highest frequency components. The first value in the vector (0) is the called the DC component and represents the lowest frequency component. The other coefficients in the vector (1 to 63) are called the AC coefficients. The 64-item vector is then passed to the quantization block for processing. In this step, each value in the 64-coefficient vector resulting from the zig-zag reordering step is divided by a predefined value and rounded to the nearest integer.

The quantization step removes the high frequency components (greater detail) of the input vector because the human eye is more sensitive to lower frequency components than higher frequency components. This is done by dividing the higher frequency coefficients in the vector by larger values than those used to divide the lower frequencies. This action forces the higher frequency components to have more zeroes. This RLC exploits the fact that we have consecutive zeroes for the higher frequency components of the input vector by providing a pair of integers indicating the number of consecutive zeroes in a run followed by the value of the nonzero number following the zeroes.

For example, consider the run of coefficients:

45, 33, 0, 0, 0, 12, 0, 0, 0, 0, 0, 0, 0, 0, 5.

The zero run-length code becomes (0,45), (0,33), (3,12), (7,5). There are special situations that are not addressed here.

Huffman coding is a process that uses a variable-length code table to map the right integer in each numbered pair generated in the previous coding step with another bit string that uses minimal space to represent the original information. This is advantageous because the variable-length code table is carefully designed to represent the most common input data patterns with shorter bit strings than for the less common input values. The result is a string of bits that is smaller in size than the original input data. The overall requirements for processing the JPEG algorithm requires only a small portion of the multicore processing capabilities. Therefore, several JPEG encoder tasks can execute on each core on multiple input video data streams.

The input data stream for a motion JPEG (MJPEG) encoder consists of a contiguous flow of raw digital images (frames). The frames are sent to the core at a particular frame rate determined on the PC. When a frame is sent to the core, the frame is partitioned into blocks of MCUs and then transmitted to an IP address defined on the network interface of the DSP. The rate at which the MCU blocks are transmitted to the DSP is predetermined and does not change regardless of the video frame rate. For this application, it is sufficient (and simpler) for a single core to manage the accelerator subsystem and service the resulting interrupts and then partition the input data block for processing by the other cores.

This is a soft real-time application because there are no hard real-time constraints. There are no imposed output frame rates at which the application must transmit the output video stream; the PC simply stalls the display of the video stream received from the DSP if the output frame rate slows below the expected rate (or stops all together). Similarly, latency is of no consequence for this application because the DSPs do not have a fixed amount of time to complete the processing. However, we will require the DSP to process the incoming data blocks as they arrive over the network interface.

6.4 SYSTEM REQUIREMENTS

Each core will process the incoming data blocks as they arrive over the network interface. Because the MCU blocks in a frame are independent, there are no restrictions on which core processes a given block. Furthermore, it is best not to assign the incoming blocks to a specific core statically, because the performance of some of the tasks in the JPEG algorithm depend on the data being processed.

6.4.1 Intercore Communication
The master core copies a pointer to the memory location of the next MCU data block to process into a global queue that is accessible by all the cores and then notifies the slave cores that there is data available for processing. All nonidle cores, including the master core, then compete to process the input block. If a core is already processing a block, it ignores the message from the master core.

The output video stream is sent over the network to a PC for decoding and display in real-time. Due to the data-dependent nature of the application JPEG algorithm, the encoded data blocks resulting from the core processing can potentially not be available in the same order as the input data blocks. This is an example of a hidden dependency on the flow order that would not exist if the application was executing on a single processor. Thus, the output data blocks must be placed in order before transmitting back to the PC. This process is called "output serialization" and is assigned to the master core. The master core must pause the output data stream from the device until the next data block in the sequence is available.

6.4.2 Master-and-Slaves Implementation

The control intelligence for the application resides in a master core. Other cores in the system become slave cores. The master core is responsible for scheduling the application processing and possibly managing the I/O. In this example a system in which Core 0 is assigned the role of master core. Core 0 manages the IO for the application and assigns tasks to the slave Cores 1, 2, and 3 via a task queue in memory. This is shown in Figure 6.5.

The key steps in getting the JPEG algorithm to run on this multicore system are:

1. Run a single instance of the JPEG application on a single core.
2. Once this functionality is properly validated, run two or more instances of the JPEG processing on the same core (this also makes debugging easier, the debugging process is simpler on one core than on multiple cores).
3. After these initial steps, the JPEG application can be executed on more than one core without any intercore communication.
4. Finally, add the intercore functionality.

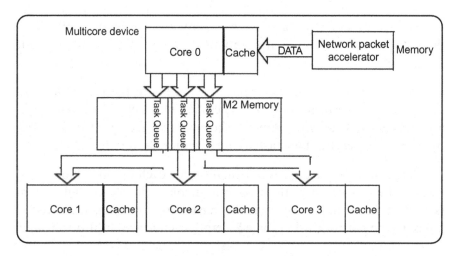

Figure 6.5 Master slave architecture for JPEG encode application.

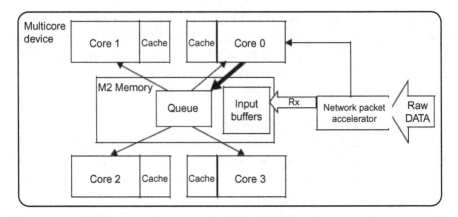

Figure 6.6 Master slave implementation with master also acting as a peer.

In the master-and-slaves scheduling implemented on the SoC for this application, the main scheduler functionality resides in Core 0, the master core. Cores 1, 2, and 3 in the system are slave cores. The master core manages the I/O and processing for the application and the slave cores wait for tasks to be processed as shown in Figure 6.6.

The incoming raw video images are received in blocks by the SoC acceleration network interface. The master core services the acceleration interrupt and then sends a message to the slave cores with the information pertinent to the received block. The slave cores are notified by messages placed in this queue which then vie to access the message and be assigned the task of JPEG encoding the video data block. If a slave core is already processing a block, it does dequeue a task until it completes the encoding of the current data block.

Core 0 (master) is notified when messages are posted to the task queue and can perform the JPEG encoding of an block if it has available processing bandwidth. Once a slave core finishes the JPEG encoding process, it notifies the master core via another message queue.

The master core dequeues information for each encoded block, and determines whether it is the next output block in the output stream (serialization). If that is the case, the master core transmits the encoded block to the network using the acceleration interface. It also transmits

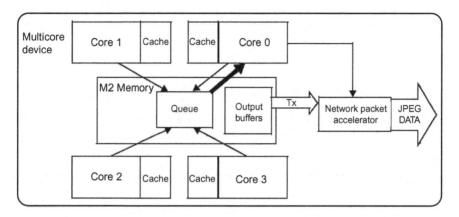

Figure 6.7 Queuing and dequeuing of video data from the network.

any additional encoded blocks that are available in the serialized sequence as shown in Figure 6.7.

If the master core performs the encoding task, it does not use the queue process, and it simply serializes the output and transmits the buffer (if possible). The core operating system (RTOS in this case) provides the basic building blocks for the scheduling of the application. In other words, the master core implements the scheduling methodology by making calls to the RTOS services through the operating system API. Similarly, the slaves respond to the master core using RTOS services. The background task in the RTOS is a user-defined function that executes when no other tasks in the application is required to execute. This task has the lowest priority and executes indefinitely in a loop until a higher priority task is enabled. The background task for this application places the corresponding core in the WAIT state by executing the wait instruction. The WAIT state is an intermediate power-saving mode used to minimize core utilization and reduce power consumption. In this case, the cores each remain in the WAIT state until a message arrives indicating a block of pixels is available for JPEG encoding, or, if it is the master core, an encoded block is ready to transmit.

The intercore communication for the application consists primarily of the messages exchanged between the master core and the slave cores. These messages are implemented in this application using services provided by the RTOS accessed through calls to the operating system API. The flow of intercore communication for the application is shown in Figure 6.8.

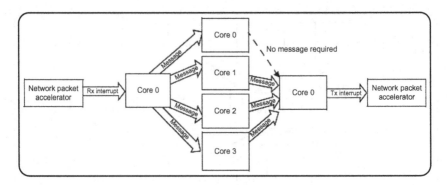

Figure 6.8 Message passing for intercore communication.

The acceleration subsystem interrupts the master core after several blocks of the raw video image are received. In the receive interrupt service routine (ISR), Core 0 sends messages to all the slave cores and to itself to indicate there is data ready for JPEG encoding. After the encoding process, the slave cores send a message back to the master core indicating there are blocks of encoded data ready to transmit. Core 0 does not need to send a message to itself. During the initialization process, each core creates queues used to send and receive messages.

The messages have two purposes. Messages from the master core (Core 0) indicate that a block of raw video data was received and is available to encode. Messages from the slave cores (Cores 1 through 3) indicate that a block has been encoded and is ready to transmit. A block encoded by Core 0 is serialized for transmission with no message generation. Messages are implemented using MSC8144 virtual interrupts between the cores. Priorities associated with the user function called when a message is received by a core are indicated below.

Data arrives to the SoC network interface from a PC over an IP network connection. The master core (Core 0) initializes and services the interrupts for the networking subsystem. Incoming data blocks are not copied. Control information is passed to the slave cores in a message with a pointer, size, and other information needed to locate the data and complete the JPEG encoding processing. The output blocks must be sent back to the PC over the IP network in the same order in which they were received. JPEG encoding processing is data

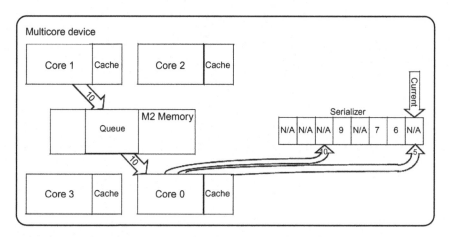

Figure 6.9 Serialization of output frames.

dependent, the cores can complete the encoding process for a block out-of-order. If the output blocks become available out of order, then the output blocks must be buffered and placed back in order, a process called output serialization. The master core executes the serialization by collecting pointers to the output buffers as they are made available by the slave cores.

Encoded buffers are then transmitted to the PC only when the next blocks in the sequential output data stream are available. In this example, the serializer shows that output blocks #6, #7, and #9 are available to be sent to the PC. However, the next block the PC is expecting is block #5 as indicated to by the Current pointer. Slave Core 1 finishes encoding output block #10 and notifies the master core which then adds it to the serializer accordingly. Core 0 then provides output block #5 which then allows blocks #5 through #7 to be sent to the PC, after which the serializer must wait for block #8 in the sequence. The serializer concept is similar to the jitter buffer used in voice over IP (VoIP) applications. The differences are that the jitter buffer in VoIP is located at the receiving end of the voice connection. This is illustrated in Figure 6.9.

CHAPTER 7

Multicore Virtualization

We discussed SMP and AMP support for multicore. AMP can implement two or more different operating systems. Unlike SMP where the operating system controls which tasks run on which core, in AMP this is not "supervised" like a SMP-aware operating system like Linux. "Unsupervised" AMP (Figure 7.1) can lead to several problems:

- Security—no enforced isolation, cannot allow untrusted operating systems
- Requires cooperation among partitions
- How are global hardware resources managed? (Local access windows, Interrupt controller, Shared caches, IOMMU)
- Boot sequence complexity
- Error management
- Resetting/rebooting partitions
- Debugging

Is there a way to "supervise" these different operating systems such that they behave? There is an approach called "virtualization" that can help with this:

- Enforcement of system security, partition boundaries
- Global resource management (e.g., interrupt controller)
- Resource sharing and virtualization—CPUs, memory, I/O devices
- Other services (e.g., debug)

The term "virtualization" stands for the process of hiding underlying physical hardware in such a way as to make it transparently usable and shareable by multiple operating systems. Actually there are many forms of virtualization technology as shown in Figure 7.2:

- Full Virtualization. This is the most flexible approach and can usually support any OS type. Full virtualization allows any legacy or new OS supported on the processor to run virtualized.

Multicore Software Development Techniques. DOI: http://dx.doi.org/10.1016/B978-0-12-800958-1.00007-3

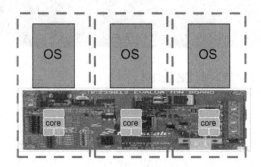

Figure 7.1 Unsupervised AMP.

This approach can be implemented with a host OS executing between the hypervisor and the hardware (but not necessarily required).

- Para Virtualization. Para virtualization will support OSs that have been modified so that it would use the virtualized layer of software's interface to communicate between the guest OSs and the virtualized layer of software. Driver modifications are usually required. Para virtualization is usually built into the host OS and then allows multiple guest OSs to execute in virtual machines. Para virtualization will usually executes faster at runtime than the full virtualization approach.
- Container Virtualization. Container virtualization technology can support OSs that have been modified to run in their virtual machine like a Para Virtualization approach. Additionally there is no attempt to virtualize the entire processor. Container virtualization implements a host OS and guest OSs for sharing the host code. The guest OSs are the same as the host OS.
- Full virtualization with hardware virtualization support. This approach leverages extensions built into the multicore hardware to support virtualization. These extensions can be in the form of I/O support, inter-VM communication support, and other optimizations. This approach is more custom to the multicore processor but also the most optimized and efficient.
- Full Virtualization with host OS. This approach can be implemented with a host OS executing between the hypervisor and the hardware.

Each instance of a guest operating system is called a virtual machine (VM), because to these VMs, the hardware is virtualized to appear as being dedicated to them.

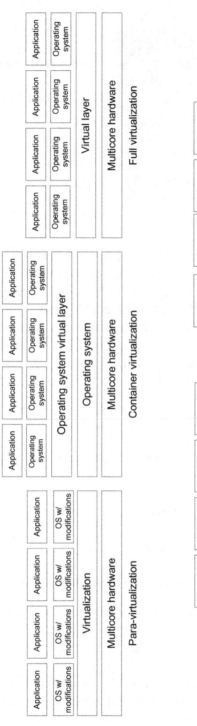

Figure 7.2 *Hypervisors add another layer of abstraction between the operating system and the physical hardware.*

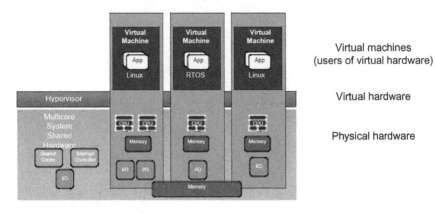

Figure 7.3 Virtualization layers.

Note that in this example, the VMs map to real hardware on the device: the VM with two cores uses two real cores on the device. It is possible for the VM to have a completely different architecture than the underlying hardware; for example, one could create a VM that thinks it is running on a four-core device when in reality there is only a single physical core (Figure 7.3). It is also possible to run multiple VMs on a single core. However, both of these options incur software overhead and are typically not seen in embedded applications.

Hypervisors provide virtualization for the following system facilities:

- CPUs (including multiple cores per device)
- Memory system (memory management and physical memory)
- I/O devices
- DMA
- Asynchronous events, such as interrupts

7.1 HYPERVISOR CLASSIFICATIONS

Hypervisors are classified into two distinct types (Figure 7.4).

- Type 1 (bare-metal) hypervisor is software that runs directly on a given hardware platform (as an operating system control program). A guest operating system thus runs at the second level above the hardware.
- Type 2 (or hosted) hypervisor is software that runs within an operating system. A "guest" operating system thus runs at the third level above the hardware.

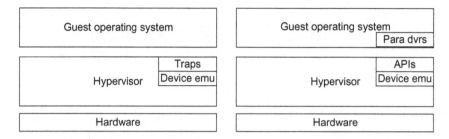

Figure 7.4 Device emulation in full virtualization (left) and para virtualization (right).

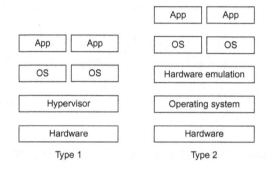

Figure 7.5 Type 1 and Type 2 hypervisors.

A hypervisor, regardless of the type, is a layered application that abstracts the machine hardware from its guests. Each guest sees a VM instead of the real hardware.

Multicore hardware continues to evolve in the area of virtualization. New processors incorporate advanced instructions to make guest operating systems and hypervisor transitions more efficient. New features for I/O virtualization also continue to evolve.

There are two different forms of virtualization (Figure 7.5);

- Full virtualization; the OS runs on a software implementation of a machine, that is, a virtual machine (VM)
- Para virtualization; A virtualization technique that presents a software interface to virtual machines that is similar, but not identical, to that of the underlying hardware. The downside to para virtualization is that the OS is aware that it is being virtualized and usually requires modifications to work.

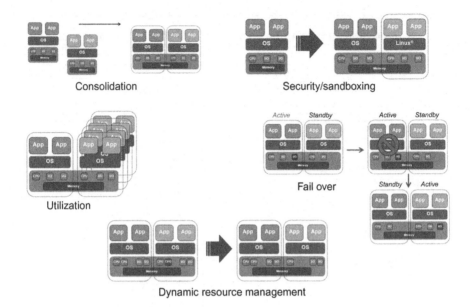

Consolidation

Security/sandboxing

Utilization

Fail over

Dynamic resource management

Figure 7.6 Virtualization use cases for multicore.

7.2 VIRTUALIZATION USE CASES FOR MULTICORE

Virtualization is used to address several multicore use cases as shown in Figure 7.6:

1. Consolidation; combining two or more separate applications and hardware devices into one multicore device
2. Security/Sandboxing; creating a dedicated Virtual Machine to "sandbox" or isolate a potentially rogue application
3. Utilization; adding more "channels" of processing in order to more fully utilize multicore resources
4. Fail over; using part of the multicore device as a backup partition in case the primary partition fails
5. Dynamic resource management; ability to use "spare" resources (cores, memory, peripherals) in the event a primary resource fails

Figure 7.7 is an example of a 3G/4G modem application that used a KVM based hypervisor in order to reduce cost by using a two core device instead of a four core device. This system was a consolidation exercise and the system was required to run an RTOS in one domain for real time processing and another RTOS along with Linux in another domain doing control processing. Instead of

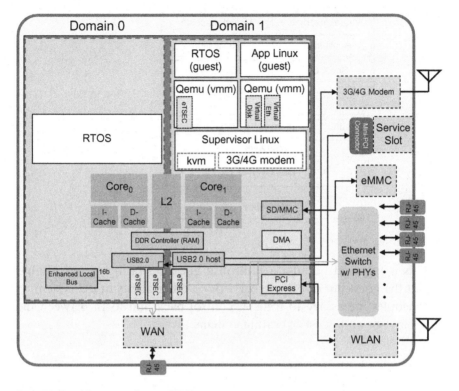

Figure 7.7 Consolidation example using KVM.

requiring three or more cores for each OS, KVM was used to virtualize one core in order to run both an RTOS and Linux on the same core. This met performance goals and also reduced cost by using fewer cores in the system.

Hypervisors implement the following key features (Figure 7.8):

- Hypercall API; allows guests to make requests of the host operating system. This is similar to system calls that bridge user-space applications with kernel functions.
- Input/output; I/O can be virtualized in the kernel or by code in the guest operating system.
- Interrupts; these can be external interrupts or interrupts for virtual devices that need to be routed to a guest operating system.
- Page mapper; the hypervisor must also handle traps or exceptions that occur within a guest. The page mapper points the hardware to the pages for the particular operating system (guest or hypervisor).

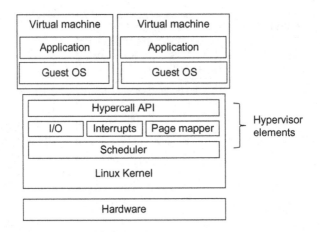

Figure 7.8 Key hypervisor elements.

This is required because a fault in a guest operating system should halt the guest but not the hypervisor or other guests in the system.

- Scheduler; necessary to transfer control back and forth between the hypervisor and guest operating systems.

7.3 LINUX HYPERVISORS

KVM (Kernel Virtual Machine) is a kernel-resident virtualization infrastructure for Linux. KVM supports symmetrical multiprocessing (SMP) hosts and guests for multicore. KVM is implemented as a kernel module, which allows Linux to become a hypervisor simply by loading a module. KVM provides full virtualization on hardware platforms that provide hypervisor instruction support.

KVM technology is implemented as two components (Figure 7.9).

- KVM-loadable module that, when installed in the Linux kernel, provides management of the virtualization hardware.
- Platform emulation component; executes as a user-space process, coordinating with the kernel for guest operating system requests. This component is referred to as QEMU (for Quick Emulator).

QEMU is an open-source based hypervisor that performs hardware virtualization. It is considered a hosted virtual machine monitor which emulates CPUs using dynamic binary translation. A set of device models is provided which allows QEMU to run different unmodified guest operating systems. QEMU is often used with KVM

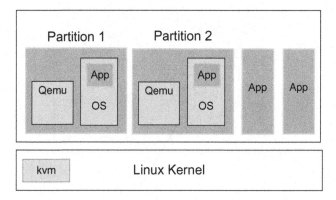

Figure 7.9 KVM components.

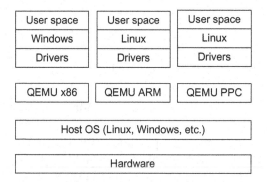

Figure 7.10 QEMU is a virtual machine monitor.

to run virtual machines (Figure 7.10). QEMU has the capability to save and restore the state of the virtual machine with all applications running. Guest operating-systems do not need patching in order to run inside QEMU.

When a system is initialized with QEMU, you can specify how many CPUs you want in the virtual machine (Virtual CPUs, VCPU in Figure 7.11). Each of these VCPUs corresponds to a Linux application level user space thread. Each of these threads interacts with KVM for services. The Linux scheduler can be used to manage these threads. Standard Linux scheduling mechanisms like CPU affinity, priorities, CPU isolation via isolcpus, and so on are possible with VCPUs.

When a new OS/VM is initialized with KVM, it becomes a process of the host operating system and is schedulable like any other process.

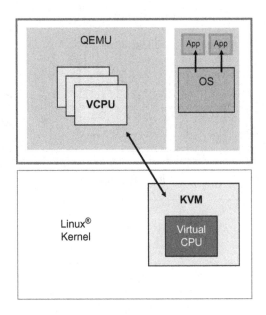

Figure 7.11 Creation of virtual CPUs (VCPUs).

Each guest OS/VM has its own virtual address space that is mapped into the host kernel's physical address space. KVM uses the hardware virtualization support to provide virtualization. I/O requests are mapped through the host kernel to the QEMU process that executes on the host (hypervisor). KVM operates as the host in Linux.

The flow of execution of a KVM based virtualization system is shown below (Figure 7.12):

1. QEMU handles initialization, initially allocates memory for the VM, loads images into memory.
2. QEMU makes API call into Linux Kernel component, KVM, to start execution of the OS.
3. KVM transfers control to the OS.
4. OS starts running, initializes, loads Apps and Apps start running. Most of the time the App will run, making occasional calls into the OS, backwards and forwards for most of the time.
5. Certain instructions designated as "privileged" will cause a trap (sometimes also called an "exit") into the KVM hypervisor (e.g., the OS tries to update the MMU, in order to provide security, the OS cannot write to memory without someone checking that it is not violating its VM rules. KVM has to validate and

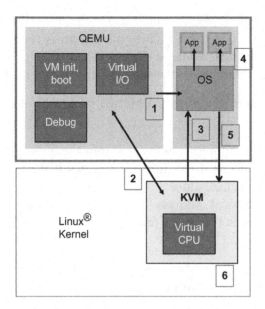

Figure 7.12 Flow of execution for KVM virtualization.

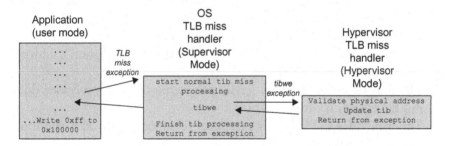

Figure 7.13 TLB miss handler.

authorize use of the MMU. Virtual I/O device interactions work in a similar way).

6. KVM handles the exit/privileged instruction and returns to the OS (the OS is unaware that this is happening).

So how does the hypervisor "take control" and process these "privileged" instructions? It has to do with different privilege layers as shown in Figure 7.13. This is an example of how to deal with a TLB miss. A translation lookaside buffer (TLB) is a memory cache that stores recent translations of virtual memory to physical addresses in order to perform fast retrieval of data. When a virtual memory address is referenced by an application, the system first checks the CPU caches. If not in these caches, the system is required to look up the memory's physical address. This is where the TLB is checked in order to get the reference to the location in physical memory.

When code is executed in a VM two stages of address translation are required:

1. A guest virtual address is translated into the guest physical address, which would be used for memory accesses if the code was run on the physical machine alone.
2. The guest physical address is translated into the host physical address, which is then used for accesses to the memory of the host machine.

This second stage of address translation is managed by the hypervisor and is transparent to the guest OS.

The steps required are listed below and in Figure 7.13.

1. The user program, running in user mode, attempts to write data to a memory location.
2. Processor checks for the requested memory address in its TLBs.
3. TLB converts this memory address from the user program's address space to VMs address space.
4. The first time this memory location is requested, the processor does not have an entry for it in TLB.
5. This generates a TLB miss exception (a supervisor-level exception), which is handled by Linux.
6. Linux, running in supervisor mode, handles the exception and runs the routines to update the TLB to point to the memory location (also determines which TLB entry can be used for the update, figures out the address translation between the VM address space and the user program's address space, and performs the TLB update).
7. tlbwe instruction generates another exception (hypervisor-level exception) that is handled by the hypervisor (because the hypervisor has a higher privilege level, it begins processing this exception before the TLB exception completes).
8. Hypervisor can do the final translation from the VM's address space to the physical address space of the device, put these values in the processor's TLB, and then return control to the VM.

There are performance considerations when using a hypervisor. The performance impact is workload dependent. The sources of CPU overhead when running under a hypervisor include:

- Privileged instructions which include TLB instructions will call an exit or trap into the hypervisor and the hypervisor will have to spend time walking through the TLB to resolve the address. This takes time.
- Privileged special purpose registers (SPR's); like the decrementer and the timer control registers.
- Hardware exceptions; such as TLB misses, Decrementer, external interrupts, instruction and data storage interrupts (ISI/DSI), etc.
- Emulated (virtual) I/O accesses.
- Hypercalls (the OS making a specific request of a hypervisor through an API call).
- Scheduling and context switches (in KVM the virtual machine is sharing the system with other tasks in the system and will get time slices with other applications in the system).

Bottom line, your mileage may vary. Be careful about using standard benchmarks to estimate virtualization overhead. A benchmark like Coremark, focusing mainly on core performance does not do many of the things in the above list (since Coremark runs out of cache, it does not stress the memory subsystem, does not cause the TLBs to be invalidated, etc) so this benchmark could be somewhat misleading. On the other hand, benchmarks that stress the MMU will show significant overhead through the hypervisor. Five to ten percent is the range that is seen often in the industry but every case is different.

7.4 VIRTUAL NETWORKING IN MULTICORE

Virtual networking in the process where physical network interfaces in the host Linux kernel (like an Ethernet port) can be shared by two or more virtual machines. Lets take an example of how to manage I/O in a multicore system. Lets assume we have two different partitions on a multicore system, each of which needs to perform I/O over a network stack to an Ethernet interface (see Figure 7.14).

There are several components to consider. In the host Linux kernel there is a physical network interface, eth0, an Ethernet port.

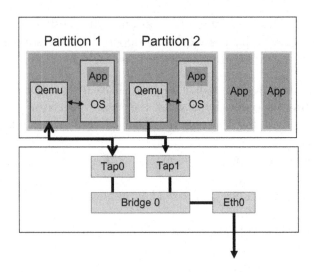

Figure 7.14 Example of virtual I/O in a multicore system.

A common way to hook up this physical network interface so that it can be shared is to use a "bridge." A bridge is a software component used to connect two or more network segments. A bridge acts like a virtual network switch. VM's using the bridge do not know or care about its existence. Any physical network interface (e.g., eth0) and virtual devices (e.g., tap0 and tap1) can be connected to it. In Figure 7.14, a bridge is connected to eth0.

When QEMU initializes a VM, it uses the tun/tap capability in Linux to connect to the bridge. tun/tap provides packet reception and transmission for user space programs in a Linux environment. "tun" (stands for network TUNnel) simulates a network layer device. tun operates with layer 3 IP packets. "tap" (stands for network tap) simulates a link layer device. tap operates with layer 2 packets like Ethernet frames. tun is used with routing, and tap is used for creating network bridges as you can see in Figure 7.14.

There is also an interface between QEMU and the guest OS as shown in Figure 7.14. From the guest OS view, it sees a virtual PCI bus (a bus that the OS can probe). On that bus are virtual network device(s). These are virtualization drivers and are referred to as "virtio" drivers. KVM provides an abstraction layer for hypervisors and a common set of I/O virtualization drivers called "virtio."

virtio provides a common front end for device emulations to standardize the interface and increase the reuse of code across platforms. virtio can be viewed as an abstraction for a set of common emulated devices in a para virtualized hypervisor (in Figure 7.4, this is the "para dvrs" box in this diagram). This approach allows the hypervisor to export a common set of emulated devices and make them available through a common application programming interface (API).

In this type of configuration, it is possible to achieve decent throughput but there will be increased latency using this approach.

7.5 I/O ACTIVITY IN A VIRTUALIZED ENVIRONMENT

I/O activity has a direct impact on performance in virtualized environments, since I/O uses interrupts for communication and synchronization. Interrupts are the main method hardware devices send asynchronous events to the operating system. The main advantage of using interrupts to receive notifications from devices instead of polling is that the processor can be freed up to perform other tasks while waiting for an interrupt. This works fine when interrupts are relatively infrequent. Each interrupt into a guest operating system has overhead, since multiple "exits" are required to handle the interrupt. For applications like storage and some networking applications, the interrupt rate is high, and the overhead of dealing with these interrupts is correspondingly high.

Figure 7.15 shows this overhead compared to base metal performance. We start with an I/O device generating an interrupt to asynchronously communicate to the CPU the completion of some I/O operation. In a virtualized environment, each interrupt causes an "exit" which causes the guest to be suspended and the host to be resumed. This happens regardless of whether or not the device is assigned. The host will first signal to the hardware the completion of the physical interrupt. The host then injects a corresponding virtual interrupt to the guest and resumes the guest's execution. The guest now has to handle the virtual interrupt. The guest will also signal completion, believing that it directly interacts with the hardware.

This triggers another exit and the host now has to emulate the completion of the virtual interrupt and then resume the guest again. These exits and context switches are overhead. For systems without a

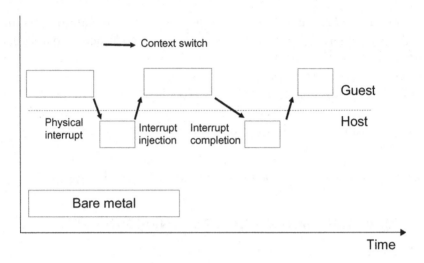

Figure 7.15 Exits during interrupt handling in a virtualized environment.

lot of I/O, this can be tolerable, but for I/O intensive operations this can be noticeable.

If we use polling we can disable the interrupt all together and check for interrupts periodically, at a rate that is acceptable to the guest OS. The downside to this approach is that we introduce added latency into the system. In some cases we can do the polling on a different core. This improves latency but we need to dedicate one of the cores to do this.

Another approach is "interrupt coalescing." In this approach, the OS programs a device to send one interrupt within a predetermined time interval or one interrupt per several events, as opposed to one interrupt for every single event. There is a latency penalty which may or may not be a concern, depending on the application.

7.6 DIRECT DEVICE ASSIGNMENT

The concept of direct device assignment improves performance of guest virtual machines by allowing them to communicate with I/O devices without involving the host. Direct device assignment is where the host assigns physical I/O devices directly to guest virtual machines. For I/O intensive devices, such as disk controllers or network cards, this can be a benefit. This can lead to improved performance because

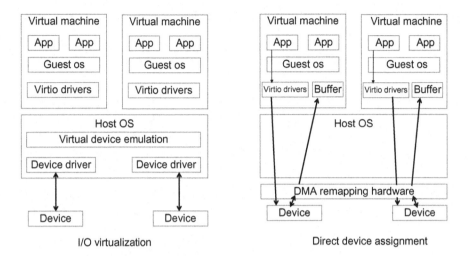

Figure 7.16 I/O virtualization versus direct device assignment.

it mostly removes the host from the guest's I/O path. Not all overhead is eliminated however. The host intercepts the interrupts generated by assigned devices in order to signal to guests the completion of their I/O requests. Because the host has to get involved, additional guest/host context switches are required, which impacts performance of I/O intensive workloads.

Figure 7.16 illustrates this. When communicating with I/O devices using virtualization, the hypervisor controls the I/O between the VMs and the device. The data gets transferred through the hypervisor layer to the device and from the device to the hypervisor layer. In the direct assignment approach, a guest OS driver controls the device it is assigned. On the receiving end, the DMA-remapping hardware layer converts the guest's physical address provided by the guest OS driver to the correct host physical address. This allows data to be transferred directly to the buffers of the guest OS. This improves performance for some applications.

CHAPTER 8

Performance and Optimization of Multicore Systems

In this chapter we will discuss optimization techniques for multicore applications. But before we begin, let's start with a quote.

Donald Knuth has said "Programmers waste enormous amounts of time thinking about, or worrying about, the speed of noncritical parts of their programs, and these attempts at efficiency actually have a strong negative impact when debugging and maintenance are considered. We should forget about small efficiencies, say about 97% of the time: premature optimization is the root of all evil."

Indeed, premature optimization as well as excessive optimization (not knowing when to stop) are harmful in many ways. Discipline and an iterative approach are the keys to effective performance tuning. The Multicore Programming Practices Guide, like many other sources of performance tuning, has its recommendation for performance tuning of multicore applications as shown in Figure 8.1.

Let's look at the top performance tuning and acceleration opportunities for multicore applications. We will focus on software related optimizations but also discuss some hardware approaches as well since they ultimately are related to software optimizations. The list we will discuss is shown below.

1. Select the right "core" for your multicore
2. Improve serial performance before migrating to multicore
3. Achieve proper load balancing (SMP Linux)
4. Improve data locality
5. Reduce or eliminate false sharing
6. Use affinity scheduling when necessary
7. Apply the proper lock granularity and frequency
8. Remove sync barriers where possible

Multicore Software Development Techniques. DOI: http://dx.doi.org/10.1016/B978-0-12-800958-1.00008-5

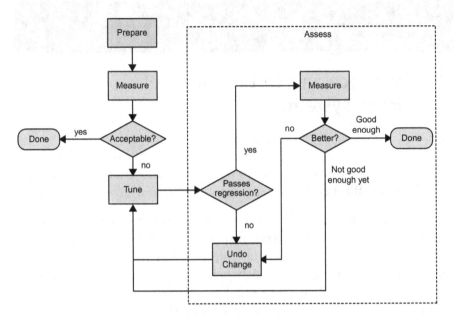

Figure 8.1 Performance tuning process from the Multicore Programming Practices Guide.

9. Minimize communication latencies
10. Use thread pools
11. Manage thread count
12. Stay out of the kernel if at all possible
13. Use parallel libraries (pthreads, openMP, etc.)

Let's explore these one by one.

8.1 SELECT THE RIGHT "CORE" FOR YOUR MULTICORE

This was the topic of Chapter 3. Do you need a latency oriented core or a throughput oriented core? Do you need hardware acceleration or not? Is a heterogeneous architecture needed or homogeneous? It makes a big difference from a performance perspective. I put this in this section as well because it makes software programming more efficient without having to resort to fancy tips and tricks to get decent performance. But it does require benchmarking and analysis of the core, the software development tools like the compiler, the operating system, etc.

8.2 IMPROVE SERIAL PERFORMANCE BEFORE MIGRATING TO MULTICORE (ESPECIALLY ILP)

Early in the development process, before looking at optimizations specific to multicore, it is necessary to spend time improving the serial (single core) application performance. Sequential execution must first be efficient before moving to parallelism to achieve higher performance. Early sequential optimization is much easier and less time consuming and less likely to introduce bugs.

Many performance improvements obtained in serial implementation will close the gap on the parallelism required to achieve your goals when moving to multicore. It is much easier to focus on parallel execution alone during this migration, instead of having to worry about both sequential and parallel optimization at the same time.

Just be careful not to introduce serial optimizations that degrade or limit parallelism, such as unnecessary data dependencies or overly exploiting details of the single core hardware architecture (such as cache capacity).

Focus on instruction level parallelism (ILP). The compiler can help. The main goal of a compiler is to maintain functionality of the application and support special functionality provided by the target and the application such as pragmas, instrinsics, and other capabilities like OpenMP which we will discuss more. For example using the "restrict" keyword (C99 standard of the C programming language) is used in pointer declarations, basically telling the compiler that for the lifetime of the pointer, only it or a value derived from it (such as pointer + 1) can be used to access an object it points to. This limits the effects of memory disambiguation or pointer aliasing which enables more aggressive optimizations. An example of this is below;

In this example, stores may alias loads. This forces operations to be executed sequentially.

```
void VectorAddition(int *a, int *b, int *c)
{
  for (int i = 0; i < 100; i++)
    a[i] = b[i] + c[i];
}
```

In this example the "restrict" keyword allows independent loads and stores. Operations can now be performed in parallel.

```
void VectorAddition(int restrict a, int *b, int *c)
{
  for (int i = 0; i < 100; i++)
    a[i] = b[i] + c[i];
}
```

The "restrict" keyword can enable more aggressive optimizations such as software pipelining. Software pipelining is a powerful loop optimization usually performed by the compiler backend. It consists of scheduling instructions across several iterations of a loop. This optimization (Figure 8.2) enables instruction level parallelism, and reduces pipeline stalls and fill delay slots. Loop iterations are scheduled so that an iteration starts before the previous iteration have completed. This approach can be combined with loop unrolling (below) to achieve significant efficiency improvements.

Loop transformations also enable ILP. Loops are typically the hotspots of many applications. Loop transformations are used to organize the sequence of computations and memory accesses to better fit the processor internal structure and enable ILP.

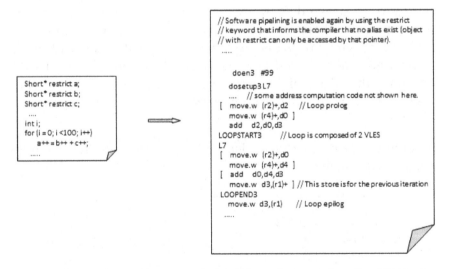

Figure 8.2 Software pipelining enables instruction level parallelism, and reduces pipeline stalls and fill delay slots.

One example of a loop transformation to enable ILP is called "loop unrolling." This transformation can decrease the number of memory accesses and improve ILP. This transformation unrolls the outer loop inside the inner loop increasing the number of independent operations inside the loop body.

Below is an example of a doubly nested loop:

```
for (i = 0; i < N; i+++)
{
  for (j = 0; j < N; j++)
  {
    a[i][j] = b[j][i] ;
  }
}
```

Here is the same loop with the loop unrolled, enabling more ILP:

```
for (i = 0; i < N; i+++)
{
  for (j = 0; j < N; j++)
  {
    a[i][j] = b[j][i] ;
    a[i+1][j] = b[j][i+1] ;
  }
}
```

This approach improves the spatial locality of "b" and increases size of loop body and therefore the available ILP. Loop unrolling also enables more aggressive optimizations, such as vectorizations (SIMD), by allowing the compiler to use these special instructions to improve performance even more, as shown in Figure 8.3, where the "move.4w"

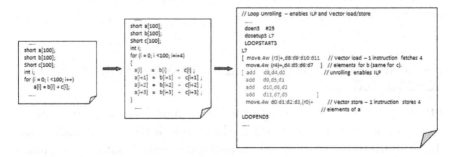

Figure 8.3 Loop unrolling can enable vectorization which improves performance even more.

instructions are essentially SIMD instructions operating on four words of data in parallel.

As with all optimizations, you need to use the right optimizations for the application. Take the example of video versus audio algorithms. For example, audio applications are based on a continuous feed of data samples. There are lots of long loops to process. This is a good application structure to use software pipelining which works well in this situation.

Video applications, on the other hand, are designed to break up video frames into smaller blocks (like the example earlier, we called this Minimal Coded Units, MCUs). This type of structure uses small loop counts and many blocks of processing. Software pipelining in this case is not as efficient due to long prologs required for pipelining. Too much overhead for each loop. In this case, it is best to use loop unrolling instead, which works better and more efficiently for these smaller loops.

Figure 8.4 shows some other basic but important serial optimizations. Using the proper word length (e.g., mapping word length to the native word length of the processor) can save cycles by preventing the processors from doing work length conversions. Using inlining functions will save cycles by eliminating function calls. Using compiler friendly instructions can save cycles by eliminating extra work to emulate nonstandard instructions or extra cycles spent on more expensive instructions. This adds up. In the example in Figure 8.4, the instruction cycle count reduces from 200 to 100 to 40 cycles as each of the above optimizations are applied.

There are many other examples of sequential optimization. The key message is to make sure you apply these first, before worrying about other parallel optimizations.

8.3 ACHIEVE PROPER LOAD BALANCING (SMP LINUX) AND SCHEDULING

Multicore aware operating systems like Linux have infrastructure to support multicore performance at the system level such as SMP schedulers, different forms of synchronization, load-balancers for interrupts, affinity scheduling techniques and CPU isolation. If used

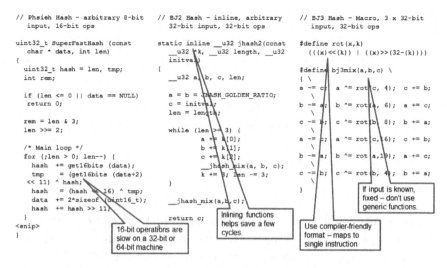

Figure 8.4 Examples of other serial optimizations (word length, inlining, and compiler friendly instructions).

properly, overall system performance can be optimized. But they all have some inherent overhead so they must be used properly.

Linux is a multitasking kernel which allows more than one process to exist at any given time. The Linux process scheduler manages which process run at any given time. The basic responsibilities are:

- share the cores equally among all currently running processes
- select the appropriate process to run next (if required), using scheduling and process priorities
- rebalance processes between multiple cores in SMP systems if necessary

Multicore applications are generally categorized to be either CPU-bound or I/O bound. CPU bound applications spend a lot of time using the CPU to do computations (like server applications). I/O bound applications spend a lot of time waiting for relatively slow I/O operations to complete (e.g., like a smart phone waiting for user input, network accesses, etc.). There is obviously a trade-off here. If we let our task run for longer periods of time, it can accomplish more work but responsiveness (to I/O) suffers. If the time period for the task gets shorter, our system can react faster to I/O event. But now more time is spent running the scheduling algorithm between task switches. This leads to more overhead and efficiency suffers.

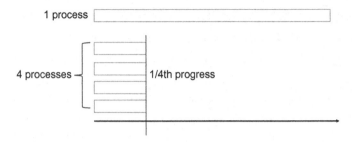

Figure 8.5 Linux completely fair scheduler (CFS).

The Linux Completely Fair Scheduler (CFS) (Figure 8.5) attempts to model a true multitasking CPU. For a system with "n" processes, the CFS attempts to schedule them at 1/n slots of the CPU. CFS uses a self balancing time ordered red-black tree algorithm.

Linux supports soft real-time policies as well as normal scheduling policies;

Soft real-time scheduling policies:

- SCHED_FIFO (FCFS, first come first served)
- SCHED_RR (real time round robin)

Normal scheduling policies (up to 40 priority levels):

- SCHED_OTHER: standard processes
- SCHED_BATCH: batch style processes
- SCHED_IDLE: low priority tasks

Linux CFS supports load balancing to improve performance of multicore SMP systems. This works by offloading tasks from busy cores to less busy or idle cores. The Linux scheduler checks periodically how the task load is spread in the system and performs load balancing if necessary. Overhead for this load balancer is controlled by adjusting the frequency of how often this operation executes which is partially dependent on the tasks in the run queues of the cores. There is a direct cost to running this operation that comes from checking the load balance of each of the cores. There is also an indirect cost that comes from potential cache invalidation (and the associated power consumption) from migrating tasks among the CPUs. Finally there is a latency cost that comes from the nonpreemptible time during the

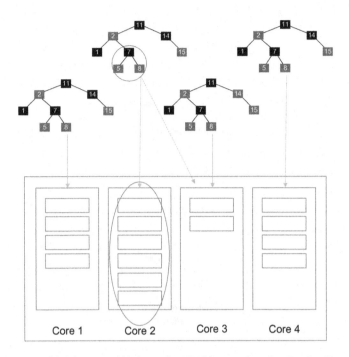

Figure 8.6 Linux CFS scheduler using red-black tree algorithm (migration from Core 2 to Core 3).

scheduling update and task migration. Obviously the amount of load balancing is application dependent.

Each CPU has a run queue. It is possible for one core to be idle while others have jobs waiting in their run queues. The scheduler periodically rebalances the run queues and locks the run queues in the same order to prevent any possible deadlock conditions (Figure 8.6).

The load balancing algorithm moves tasks from busy run queues to idle run queues. If the scheduler finds a run queue with no runnable tasks, it calls the load balancer. The load balancer can also be called (via a timer) from two system heartbeats; the scheduler tick and the rebalancing tick.

The load balancer will search for the busiest core run queue (the one with the most runnable tasks) and remove a task that is (in order of preference):

- inactive (most likely these also have cold caches)
- high priority tasks

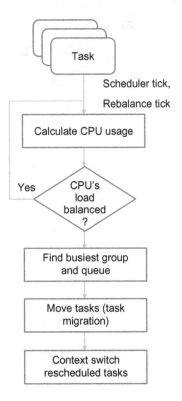

Figure 8.7 SMP load balancing in Linux.

The load balancer will skip tasks that:

- have warm caches
- are currently running on a core
- are not allowed to run on the current core (this is set using the cpus_allowed bitmask in the task_struct)

The devil is in the details. There are a variety of different SMP system topologies. Some systems have multiple physical cores and tasks may suffer from cache flushes that occur when processes are moved from a busy CPU to a less busy one. NUMA systems and hyper threaded systems have inherent complexities that must be managed. For example NUMA architectures have multiple nodes with different access times to different areas of main memory. Linux supports NUMA by using something called "scheduling domains" which is a way to hierarchically group the available CPUs in the system and provides the kernel a way of characterizing the system core topology (Figure 8.7).

8.4 IMPROVE DATA LOCALITY

This has been discussed earlier as well, but there are some additional comments to be made concerning software optimizations related to data locality. This is a key focus area for multicore optimization. In many applications, this requires some careful analysis of the application. For example, let's consider a networking application that using the Linux operating system.

In the Linux operating system, all network-related queues and buffers use a common data structure called "sk_buff." This is a large data structure that holds all of the control information needed for a network packet. The sk_buff structure elements are organized as a doubly linked list. This allows efficient movement of sk_buff elements from the beginning/end of a list to the beginning/end of another list.

The standard skbuff has information spread over three or more cache-lines. Data-plane applications require only one cacheline worth of information.

We can take advantage of this by creating a new structure that packs/aligns to a single cache line. If we are smart and make this part of the packet buffer headroom. Now we don't have to worry about cache misses and flushes each time we access the large sk_buff structure, instead we use a small portion of this that fits neatly into cache, improving data locality and efficiency. This is shown in Figure 8.8.

8.5 REDUCE OR ELIMINATE FALSE SHARING

False sharing occurs when two software threads manipulate data that are on the same cache line. As we have discussed earlier, the memory system of a multicore processor must ensure cache coherency in SMP systems. Any modifications made to shared cache must be flagged to the memory system so each processor is aware the cache has been modified. The affected cache line is "invalidated" when one thread has changed data on that line of cache. When this happens the second thread must wait for the cache line to be reloaded from memory (Figure 8.9).

The code below shows this condition. In this example, sum_temp1 may need to continually re-read "a" from main memory (instead of from cache) even though inc_b's modification of "b" should be irrelevant.

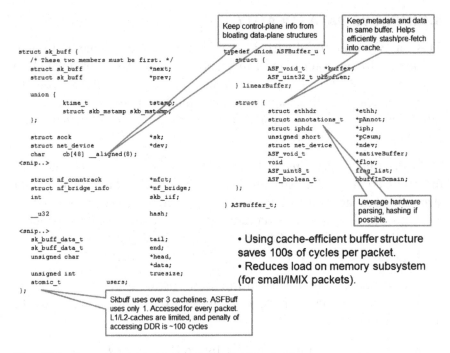

Figure 8.8 Creating an efficient data structure to improve locality and performance.

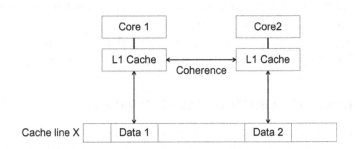

Figure 8.9 False sharing in SMP systems.

In this situation, if the extra prefetched words are not needed and another processor in this cache-coherent, shared memory system must immediately change these words, this extra transfer has a negative impact on system performance and energy consumption.

```
struct data
{
  volatile int a;
  volatile int b;
} ;
```

```
data f;
int sum_temp1()
{
  int s = 0;
  for (int i = 0; i < 1000; i++)
    s + = f.a;
  return s;
}
void inc_b()
{
  for (int i = 0; i < 1000; i++)
    ++f.b;
}
```

One solution to this condition is to pad the data in the data structure so that the elements caching false sharing performance degradation will be allocated on different cache lines.

```
struct data                          struct data
{                                    {
      volatile int a;                     volatile int a;
      volatile int b;                     unsigned char
                                          padding[CACHE_LINE__SIZE – sizeof(int)];
};                                        volatile int b;
                                     };
```

8.6 USE AFFINITY SCHEDULING WHEN NECESSARY

In some applications it might make sense to force a thread to stay executing on a particular core instead of letting the operating system make the decision whether or not to move the thread to another core. This is referred to as "processor affinity." Operating systems like Linux have APIs to allow a developer to control this. This allows them the ability to map certain threads to cores in a multicore processor (Figure 8.10).

On many processor architectures, any migration of threads across cache, memory, or processor boundaries can be expensive (flushing the cache, etc.). The developer can use APIs to set affinities for certain threads to take advantage of shared caches, interrupt handing, and to match computation with data (locality). A snippet of code that shows how to do this is below:

```
#define _GNU_SOURCE
#include <sched.h>
```

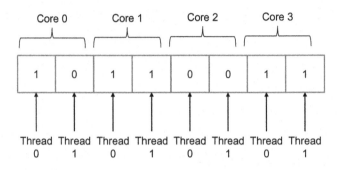

Figure 8.10 Process affinity.

```
long
sched_setaffinity(pid_t pid, unsigned int len,
         unsigned long *user_mask_ptr);
long
sched_getaffinity(pid_t pid, unsigned int len,
         unsigned long *user_mask_ptr);
```

In the code snippet above, the first system call will set the affinity of a process. The second system call retrieves the affinity of a process.

The PID argument is the process ID of the process you want to set or retrieve. The second argument is the length of the affinity bitmask. The third argument is a pointer to the bitmask. Masks can be used to set affinity of the cores of interest.

If you set the affinity to a single CPU this will exclude other threads from using that CPU. This also takes that processor out of the pool of resources that the OS can allocate. Any time you are manually controlling affinity scheduling, be careful. There may be side affects that are not obvious. Design the affinity scheduling scheme carefully to ensure efficiency.

8.7 APPLY THE PROPER LOCK GRANULARITY AND FREQUENCY

There are two basic laws of concurrent execution;

1. The program should not malfunction
2. Concurrent execution should not be slower than serial execution

We use locks as a mutual exclusion mechanism to prevent multiple threads' simultaneous access to shared data or code sections. These locks are usually implemented using semaphores or mutexes which are essentially expensive API calls into the operating system

Locks can be fine-grained or coarse-grained. Too many locks increases the amount of time spent in the operating system and also increases the risk of deadlock. Coarse-grained locking reduces the chance of deadlock but can cause additional performance degradations due to locking large areas of the application (mainly system latency).

Avoiding heavy use of locks and semaphores due to performance penalties. Here are some guidelines:

- Organize global data structures into buckets and use a separate lock for each bucket.
- Design the system to allow threads to compute private copies of a value and then synchronize only to produce the global result. This will require less locking.
- Avoid spinning on shared variables waiting for events.
- Use atomic memory read/writes to replace locks if the architecture supports this.
- Avoid atomic sections when possible (an atomic section is a set of consecutive statements that can only be run by one thread at a time).
- Place locks only around commonly used fields and not entire structures if this is possible.
- Compute all possible pre- and post calculations outside of the critical section, as this will minimize time spent in a critical section.
- Make sure that locks are taken in the same order to prevent deadlock situations.
- Use mechanisms that are designed to reduce overhead in the operating system. For example, in POSIX-based systems, use the trylock() function that allows the program to continue execution to handle an unsuccessful lock. In Linux use the "futex" (fast user space mutex) to do resource checks in user space instead of the kernel (see below).

8.8 REMOVE SYNC BARRIERS WHERE POSSIBLE

A synchronization barrier causes a thread to wait until the other threads have reached the barrier and are used to ensure that variables needed at a given execution point are ready to be used. They are different than a lock for this reason (Figure 8.11).

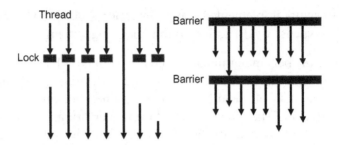

Figure 8.11 Locks versus barriers.

Barriers can have the same performance problem as locks if not used properly. Over-synchronizing can negatively impact performance. For this reason, barriers should be used only to ensure that data dependencies are respected and/or where the execution frequency is the lowest.

A barrier can be used to replace creating and destroying threads multiple times when dealing with a sequence of tasks (i.e., replacing join and create threads), so when used in this way, certain performance improvements can be realized.

8.9 MINIMIZE COMMUNICATION LATENCIES

When possible, limit communication in multicore systems. In many cases, even extra computing is often more efficient than communication. For example, one approach to minimize communication latencies is to distribute data by giving each CPU has its own local data set that it can work on. This is called "per-cpu data" and is a technique used in the Linux kernel for several critical subsystems. For example, the kernel slab allocator uses per-cpu data for fast CPU local memory allocation. The disadvantage is higher memory overhead and increased complexity dealing with CPU hotplug.

In general the communication time can be estimated using the following:

$$T_{com}(n) = \alpha + \beta * n$$

where

- n, size of the message
- α, the startup time due to the latency
- β, the time for sending one data unit limited by the available bandwidth

Here are a few other tips and tricks to reduce communication latency:

- Gather small messages into larger ones when possible to increase the effective communications bandwidth (reduce β, reduce α, increase n).
- Sending noncontiguous data is usually less efficient than sending contiguous data (increases α, decreases n).
- Do not use messages that are too large. Some communication protocols change when messages get too large (increases α, increases n, increases β).
- The layout of processes/threads on cores may affect performance due to the communication network latency and the routing strategy (increases α).
- Use asynchronous communication techniques to overlap communication and computation. Asynchronous communication (nonblocking) primitives do not require the sender and receiver to "rendezvous" (decrease α).
- Avoid memory copies for large messages by using zero-copy protocols (decrease β).

8.10 USE THREAD POOLS

When using a peer or master/worker design as discussed earlier, users should not create new threads on the fly. This causes overhead. Instead have them stopped when they are not being used. Creating and freeing processes and threads is expensive. The penalty caused by the associated overhead may be larger than the benefit of running the work in parallel.

In this approach, a number of threads are allocated to a thread "pool." N threads are created to perform a number of operations, M, where N $<<$ M. When a threads completes a task it is working on, it will then request the next task from the thread pool (usually organized into a queue) until all of the tasks have been completed. The thread can then terminate (or sleep) until there are new tasks that become available. Figure 8.12 shows a conceptual diagram of this.

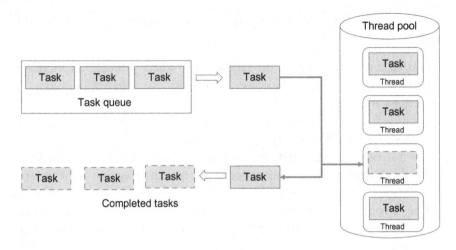

Figure 8.12 Thread pool concept.

A thread pool is implemented as a data structure as shown below:

```
typedef struct _threadpool{
    int num_threads;            //number of active threads
    int qsize;                  // queue size
    pthread_t *threads;         //pointer to threads
    work_t* qhead;              //queue head pointer
    work_t* qtail;              //queue tail pointer
    pthread_mutex_t qlock;      //lock on the queue list
    pthread_cond_t q_not_empty; //non empty and empty condidtion vairiables
    pthread_cond_t q_empty;
    int shutdown;
    int dont_accept;
} thread_pool;
```

The associated C code can be implemented to control access to the thread pools data structure. This is not shown here but there are plenty of examples you can find that show reference implementations.

8.11 MANAGE THREAD COUNT

As discussed in Chapter 3, parallel execution always incurs some overhead resulting from functions such as task start-up time, inter-task synchronization, data communications, hardware bookkeeping (e.g., memory consistency), software overhead (libraries, tools, runtime system, etc.), and task termination time.

As a general rule, small tasks (fine grain) are usually inefficient due to the overhead to manage many small tasks. Large tasks could lead to load imbalance. In many applications, there is a tradeoff between having enough tasks to keep all cores busy and having enough computation in each task to amortize the overhead.

The optimal thread count can also be determined by estimating the average blocking time of the threads running on each core:

Thread count = number of cores/

(1 − perentage average blocking time of threads)

8.12 STAY OUT OF THE KERNEL IF AT ALL POSSIBLE

We gain a lot of support from operating systems but when optimizing for performance it is sometimes better to not go in and out of the operating system often, as this incurs overhead. There are many tips and tricks for doing this so study the manual for the operating system and learn about the techniques available to optimize performance. For example, Linux supports SMP multicore using mechanisms like "futex" (fast user space mutex).

A futex is comprised of two components:

- a kernelspace wait queue
- an integer in userspace.

In multicore applications, the multiple processes or threads operate on the integer in userspace and only use expensive system calls when there is a need to request operations on the wait queue (Figure 8.13). This would occur if there was a need to wake up waiting processes, or put the current process on the wait queue. Futex operations do not use system calls except when the lock is contended. But since most operations do not require arbitration between processes, this will not happen in most cases (Figure 8.14).

8.13 USE PARALLEL LIBRARIES (PTHREADS, OPENMP, ETC.)

For larger multicore applications, attempting to implement the entire application using threads is going to be difficult and time consuming. An alternative is to program atop a concurrency platform. Concurrency

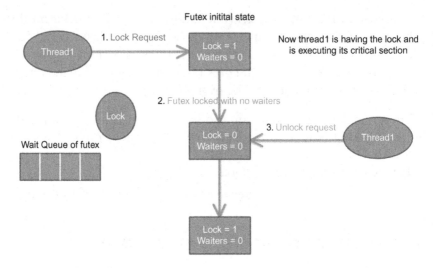

Figure 8.13 A futex prevents calls into the kernel.

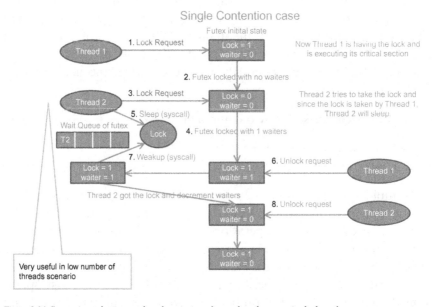

Figure 8.14 Contention only occurs when there is a need to update the queue in the kernel.

platforms are abstraction layers of software that coordinate, schedule, and manage multicore resources. This is the topic of Chapter 10 but it is mentioned here as well because using concurrency platforms such as OpenMP, Thread building libraries, OpenCL, etc. can not only speed time to market but also help with system level performance. It may seem counterintuitive to use abstraction layers to increase performance but these concurrency platforms provide frameworks that prevent the developer from making mistakes that could lead to performance problems. We will talk more about the details in Chapter 10.

Let's consider another example of a multicore application and this time we will focus on how to optimize it and make it run faster.

To do so we will examine the performance costs of workload allocation, synchronization and threading overhead, and data locality.

We will also briefly touch on some sequential optimization where applicable.

In order to illustrate these concepts we will be improving a very poor multithreaded implementation of the cellular automaton simulation: Conway's Game of Life.

Before we dive into examining our application performance, let's briefly review how the Game of Life works. The Game of Life consists of a rectangular grid (we'll simplify this to a square of n by n size) where each cell may or may not be "populated" by "life." This means that each cell of our grid will either have life (true or 1) or not (false or 0). The grid is seeded at startup with a scattering of various "life" and in each iteration the rules of "life" are applied to each cell, determining who "lives," "dies," or is "born." The rules of "life" are as follows:

1. Any live cell with fewer than two live neighbors dies, as if caused by underpopulation.
2. Any live cell with two or three live neighbors lives on to the next generation.
3. Any live cell with more than three live neighbors dies, as if by overcrowding.
4. Any dead cell with exactly three live neighbors becomes a live cell, as if by reproduction

By applying these rules to the grid with each iteration we simulate Conway's Game of Life.

The code for this application is shown in Appendix A (Conway's Game of Life Unoptimized). There is an unoptimized code and an optimized code. Let's walk through how to get from one to the other.

If you run this application on a 4 core multicore processor you would notice that the execution time goes as the number of threads increases. Why would that be? Clearly, there is something wrong with this multithreaded implementation. The code for the "Game of Life" application is shown in Appendix A, starting on line 1, page 202.

The thread creation process starts on line 177, page 206. What do you first notice about the use of threads? They are allocated and joined per iteration! That is a lot of threading overhead to induce per iteration. This rampant creation and deletion of threads is surely not necessary, but we will come back to that later. For now, note the general structure of the algorithm: each iteration keep a record of the "next" cell in the grid to be computed, then create and start threads and share the "next" cell value with them. Finally the main thread will be waiting while joining the other threads. Rinse and repeat for every iteration of the game.

Now that we know how the main thread works let's look at the other threads. In **gol.c** look at the **compute_cells** function starting on line 208, page 207. Here we see that each thread is continuously checking a shared variable (**int * next_cell**) to know which cell to compute, repeating until collectively the threads complete all the cells in the grid. Notice, however, that this check is inside of a critical section. This makes sense, otherwise there would be a race condition between each thread over evaluating the value and incrementing. However, having a critical section in such a frequently executed piece of code is very detrimental to performance. For every cell, in every iteration of the Game of Life, our threads need to sequentially wait on each other to know what cell to compute next. What makes this even worse is that the evaluation process for each cell is trivial and likely shorter than the process of waiting for, acquiring, and releasing the lock. Clearly this thread pool pattern applied here is not the best choice for an effective parallel implementation, much less an optimal one.

So how can we improve this multicore program? Minimizing the number and duration of critical sections is usually a good place to start when optimizing a parallel program. Let's start by trying to eliminate our critical section around accessing and incrementing **next_cell**. This is shown in lines 222 through 233, page 207. Unfortunately, this critical section is vital to prevent a race condition around variable, so let's rethink our algorithm. Can we change the way we distribute work to remove the need for this critical section? It turns out we can.

Since the number of cells in our grid is static we can assign cells to each thread ahead of time, removing the need for our threads to communicate this information. Now that we will no longer need to negotiate work between threads we can eliminate the critical section in **compute_cells** and therefore reduce some of our communication overhead.

We can make the following changes to **gol.c**:

- Modify the **thread_args** structure starting on line 43, page 203. Replace the **next_cell** and **next_cell_lock** variables with integers **start_cell** and **cells_to_compute**. These values will tell the thread which cell to start with and how many to compute.
- Next we need to update the **parallel_game_of_life** function (line 19, page 203) so that the **thread_args** reflects these changes. We need to calculate these values for each thread so the workload is distributed evenly. We must also account for when the cells don't divide evenly across threads! You can give any remainder to the last thread. We'll delete all of the references to **next_cell_lock** and **next_cell**.
- Finally we need to change the **compute_cells** function (line 208, page 207) to reflect these changes. We'll delete all references to **total_cells**, **current_cell**, **next_cell**, and **next_cell_lock**. In their place, let's use the new thread arguments **start_cell** and **cells_to_compute** and iterate over and compute all of the cells between **start_cell** and **start_cell + cells_to_compute**. Note that, per iteration, we will need to update **next_cell_row** and **next_cell_column** (the math remains the same).

Now that we have removed our performance- killing critical section, let's change the way we manage our threads so we don't have the overhead of constantly creating and deleting threads each iteration. Instead, let's have our main thread simply create the threads and then wait for them to join. This requires passing the responsibility of iterating and synchronizing to each thread.

This requires us to make the following changes:

In the function **parallel_game_of_life** we will remove the **for** loop iterating over **g_iterations**. Also, let's remove the section that uses **bool ** tmp** to swap the boards. Finally, we will get rid of the **if** statement of **g_display** that is responsible for printing the board. All of this logic will be relocated to the worker thread(s).

Now we need to go to the function compute_cells and reintroduce the logic we just removed: we add an outer loop around where we iterate over the cells. This loop should repeat the cell computation loop for the number of iterations, g_iterations. We also need to swap our boards and do the grid display after each iteration is complete:

```
bool ** tmp = cb;
cb = ib;
ib = tmp;
if (g_display) {
//The first thread will handle any printing.
if (start_cell == 0) {
print_board(ib, g_rows, g_columns);
sleep(1);
}
}
```

Great! Now our program will only create and destroy threads at the beginning and end of its execution.

However, we have introduced a race condition into our code! Previously the creation/destruction of our threads was forcing us to synchronize between iterations, but now that is not happening. We need to add a mechanism to have our threads synchronize after computing the cell values every iteration. What we need is a **barrier**.

As discussed earlier, barriers are used to synchronize threads, as a thread will not progress beyond a barrier until **all** other threads have reached the barrier. This is exactly what we need here in our iterative method!

To add our synchronization barrier to our code, let's make these changes (this optimized code is shown in Appendix A starting on line 1, page 209):

- First, we add another field to our **thread_args** structure of type **struct simple_barrier** *.
- Then in our main thread, in the function **parallel_game_of_life**, we create a **struct simple_barrier** on the heap. Then, call **simple_barrier_init** with our new barrier and the number of threads as the arguments.

```
struct simple_barrier * barrier = (struct simple_barrier*)
   malloc(sizeof(struct simple_barrier));
simple_barrier_init(barrier, g_threads);
```

- Next, we assign this newly created pointer to each structure of thread arguments we create.
- Finally, in the **compute_cells** function, we will call **simple_barrier_wait** after computing the cells and swapping the boards for each iteration. We pass the barrier pointer from the **thread_args** as the argument to **simple_barrier_wait**.

All of this is shown in Appendix A, "Conway's Game of Life Optimized" starting on line 1, page 209.

At this point we have a scalable, multithreaded Game of Life simulation with reasonably good spatial data locality. So what else can we do to improve application performance? There is little to do in terms of optimization of synchronization patterns, as the Game of Life itself is an iterative method. Instead, let's examine the serial segments of our code that each thread executes. What can we optimize there?

Plenty is the answer. To convert the raw cell count to row and column indices for accessing our 2D matrix we use both the division and modulo operators which are very expensive computationally. Additionally, the way we check our cell's neighbors can be improved. Currently, we have a set of 8 conditionals that evaluate if our neighbors are alive. These branch statements can be somewhat costly to compute and fortunately there is a quick and easy optimization we can do here. Because the value of each neighbor is either 1 or 0 and we are incrementing **value** for every neighbor that is set 1, we can simply sum the neighbors instead.

So let's make these serial optimization changes:

In the **compute_cells** function starting on line 241, page 208, we can replace the 8 **if** statements checking the cell neighbors with a single statement summing the values of the 8 neighbors into the **value** variable.

The other optimization, removing the division and modulo operations, is a bit more involved. Instead of giving each thread a cell range, let's instead divide the work into rows and assign each thread one of these sets of rows, allowing us to avoid doing more expensive arithmetic operations inside our inner loop. This will, again, require modifying the thread arguments structure **thread_args**.

Rename the two integers, **start_cell** and **cells_to_compute**, in the **thread_args** structure to **start_row** and **end_row**, respectively. Then we apply this name change through the **parallel_game_of_life** function and into the **compute_cells** function.

Now we update the logic in **parallel_game_of_life** to reflect these changes in structure. When calculating the starting and ending row for each thread, we are careful to keep in mind that our grid has a 1 cell wide "dead" zone boundary on each side.

Finally, we will update the **compute_cell** function to extract these new values from the **thread_args** structure and then use them to iterate over the cells in a nested loop. We are careful to iterate in row-major order! All of these changes and optimizations are shown in the code in Appendix A starting on line 1, page 209

Check out the results shown in the bar chart in Figure 8.15. What an improvement! By changing our algorithm to remove critical sections we have made a tremendously faster and more scalable solution. One added benefit of this change is that, in addition to removing a critical section, we also force our threads to operate on contiguous cell groups. This greatly improves the spatial data locality of our program and helps improve performance!

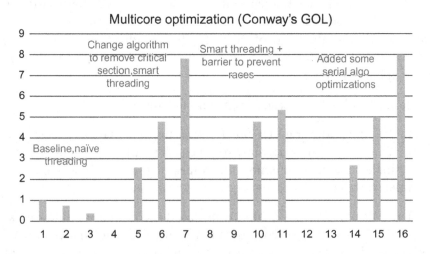

Figure 8.15 Optimizations for Conway's Game of Life, improving optimizations with different thread counts.

Let's consider another example, the computation of primes using a multicore processor.

The first question is how to separate the workload for parallel execution? As in matrix multiplication, you could simply divide the workload into distinct chunks—which in this case means dividing the search space into 2 chunks (let's keep it simple for starters and just think in terms of 2 threads). Take a look at the "Primes" code in Appendix A starting on line 1, page 189.

You can try this, but it is not a good approach... Why not? Because one thread will have the smaller numbers, and the other thread will have the longer numbers. And since the **isPrime** test function is loop-based (Appendix A, line 116, page 192), the larger the number the longer it takes to test for "primeness." So one thread will finish much sooner than the other. Not a good distribution of workload—poor load balancing.

A common solution to the above problem is to "stride" through the data, i.e., one thread does the even numbers and one thread does the odd numbers (or given 4 threads, one thread does x, x + 4, x + 8, ..., while the next thread does x + 1, x + 5, x + 9, ..., and so on).

What is the problem there? Well, the thread doing the even numbers will zip through the search space, since even numbers are never prime! Once again not a very good distribution of the workload in this case.

Analyze the "Primes" code and look at the **AddToList** function starting on line 150, page 192. Any multiply threads calling "**AddToList**" in parallel will have a race condition since the list is a shared resource, and cannot be safely updated in parallel. This implies the call to **AddToList** is a critical section, and should be surrounded by a pthread_mutex_lock/ pthread_mutex_unlock.

We can fix this and we did in the "Improved Primes" code in Appendix A starting on line 1, page 195.

This improved code shows a **_DoPrimeNumberSearch** (starting on line 161, page 198) that takes 2 arguments: the *end* of the search space, and a pointer to a long that denotes the next *candidate* number to test for "*primeness.*" We implemented this function to loop forever: (i) grabbing the next candidate value, (ii) advancing the candidate so

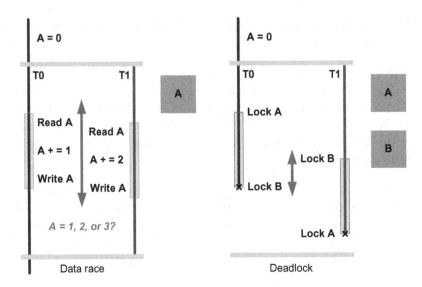

Figure 8.16 Data races and deadlocks can occur in multicore systems.

there are no dups, (iii) checking to see if this candidate value is > end (in which case exit the loop), otherwise (iv) checking to see if the candidate value is prime—and if so, adding it to the list. Repeat. When the loop ends, return NULL.

So what happened? The most obvious error is that you having multiple threads trying to add primes to the list, which is a shared resource. This yields a race condition that ultimately crashes the program since pointers are involved (see Figure 8.16). Data structures are a common source of race conditions, since they are generally hidden behind function calls—e.g., **AddToList**—and so it is easy to forget there are shared variables involved.

The easiest solution is to create a **mutex** ("lock") in the **PrimeNumberSearch** function, and then pass a pointer to this lock to each of the threads. The threads must then use this lock to protect access to the list. In particular, surround the call to **AddToList** with **pthread_mutex_lock** and **pthread_mutex_unlock** (lines 192−194, page 199 in Appendix A:

```
pthread_mutex_lock( ptr_to_lock );
AddToList(p);
pthread_mutex_unlock( ptr_to_lock );
```

The good news is that the program will no longer crash. The bad news is that it is not correct—the program as written will report duplicate primes... Why? There is another race condition, in this case with the *candidate* variable—this is a shared resource being accessed, in particular read and written—by both threads. Those R and W accesses form a critical section, which needs at the very least to be protected by a lock.

Once again, the easiest solution is to create another lock in the **PrimeNumberSearch** function (lines 131–133, page 198 and lines 177–180 on pages 198 and 199), pass a pointer to this lock to the threads, and have the threads use this lock to protect the read and write of the *candidate* value.

The "fixed" Primes code is shown in Appendix A (line 1, page 195).

CHAPTER 9

Sequential to Parallel Migration of Software Applications

In this chapter we will take a look at the process and steps to convert a sequential software application to a multicore application. There are many legacy sequential applications that may be converted to multicore. This chapter shows the steps to do that.

Figure 9.1 is the process used to convert a sequential application to a multicore application.

9.1 STEP 1: UNDERSTAND REQUIREMENTS

Of course the first step is to understand the key functional as well as nonfunctional (performance, power, memory footprint, etc.) for the application. When migrating to multicore, should the results be bit exact or is the goal equivalent functionality? Scalability and maintainability requirements should also be considered. Keep in mind, that when migrating to multicore, good enough is good enough. We are not trying to over achieve, just because we have multiple cores to work with.

9.2 STEP 2: SEQUENTIAL ANALYSIS

In this step we want to capture design decisions and learnings. Start from a working sequential code base. Then iteratively refine implementation. Explore the natural parallelism in the application. In this phase it also makes sense to tune implementation to target platform. Move from stable state to stable state to ensure you do not break anything. Follow these steps:

- Start with optimized code
- Ensure libraries are thread safe

Multicore Software Development Techniques. DOI: http://dx.doi.org/10.1016/B978-0-12-800958-1.00009-7

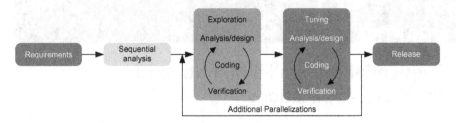

Figure 9.1 A process flow from a sequential application to a parallel application.

- Profile to understand the structure, flow, and performance of the application
  - Attack hotspots first
  - Select optimal cut points (a cut-set of a program is a set of locations (called cut-points) such that each cycle in the control flow graph of the program passes through some program location in the cut-set)

9.3 STEP 3: EXPLORATION

In this step, we explore different parallelization strategies. The best approach is to use quick iterations of analysis/design, coding, and verification. We aim to favor simplicity over performance. Remember to have a plan for verification of each iteration so you do not regress. The key focus in this step is on dependencies and decomposition.

9.4 STEP 4: CODE OPTIMIZATION AND TUNING

The Tuning step involved the identification and optimization of performance issues. These performance issues can include:

- Thread stalls
- Excessive synchronization
- Cache thrashing

Iteration and experimentation are the keys to this step in the process. Examples of experiments to try are:

- Vary threads and the number of cores
- Minimize locking
- Separate threads from tasks

Figure 9.2 Edge detection pipeline.

9.5 IMAGE PROCESSING EXAMPLE

Let's explore this process in more detail by looking at an example. We will use an image processing example shown in Figure 9.2. We will use an Edge Detection Pipeline for this example.

A basic sequential control structure for the edge detection example is shown below;

```
static void *edge_detect(void *argv) {
   ed_arg_t *arg = (ed_arg_t *)argv;;
   char unsigned *out_pixels, *in_pixels;
   int col0, cols, nrows, ncols;

   unpack_arg(arg, &out_pixels, &in_pixels, &col0, &cols, &nrows, & ncols);

   correct(out_pixels, in_pixels, col0, cols, nrows, ncols);
   smooth(in_pixels, out_pixels, col0, cols, nrows, ncols);
   detect(out_pixels, in_pixels, col0, cols, nrows, ncols);

   return NULL;
}
```

Let's now work through the steps we discussed earlier so see how we can apply this approach to this example. We will start with step two, "Sequential Analysis."

9.6 STEP 2: SEQUENTIAL ANALYSIS

Figure 9.3 shows that the three processing steps are unbalanced from a total processing load. The "Smooth" function dominates the processing, followed by the "Detect" function, and then the "Correct" function. By looking at the code above we can also come to the conclusion that each function is embarrassingly data parallel. There is constant work per pixel in this algorithm, but also very different amounts of work per function, as you can see in Figure 9.3. This is also the time to make sure that you are only using thread safe C libraries in this function, as we will be migrating this to multicore software using threads.

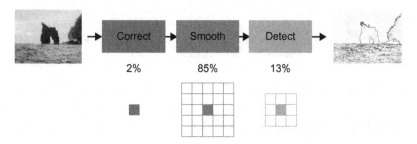

Figure 9.3 Exploration phase of edge detection algorithm showing a profile of processing steps.

9.7 STEP 3: EXPLORATION

As mentioned previously, this is the step where we explore different parallelization strategies, such as:

• Quick analysis/design, coding, and verification iterations
• Favor simplicity over performance
• Verify each iteration
• Focus on dependencies and decomposition granularity

We decompose to expose parallelism. Keep in mind these rules:

• Prioritize hotspots
• Honor dependencies
• Favor data decomposition

Remember we may also need to "Recompose" (we sometimes call this agglomeration) considering:

• Workload granularity and balance
• Platform and memory characteristics

During exploration, do not overthink it. Focus on the largest, least interdependent chunks of work to keep N cores active simultaneously. Use strong analysis and visualization tools to help you (there are several of them we will talk about later).

9.8 STEP 4: OPTIMIZATION AND TUNING

For this example we will follow these important rules of thumb during the optimization and tuning phase:

• Follow good software engineering practices
• Code incrementally

Figure 9.4 Parallel execution of the edge detection pipeline algorithm on two cores.

- Code in order of impact
- Preserve scalability
- Don't change two things at once

In this phase, you must also verify changes often. Remember, parallelization introduces new sources of error. Reuse sequential tests for functional verification even though the results may not be exact due to computation order differences. Check for common parallelization errors such as data races and deadlock. Perform stress testing where you change both the data as well as the scheduling at the same time. Perform performance bottleneck evaluation.

9.9 DATA PARALLEL; FIRST ATTEMPT

The strategy for attempt one is to partition the application into "N" threads, one per core. Each thread handles *width/N* columns. The different image regions are interleaved. We create a thread for each slice as shown in the code below, line 10, and then join them back together in line 13. A picture of how this is partitioned is shown in Figure 9.4.

```
1 void *edge_detect(char unsigned *out_pixels, char unsigned
*in_pixels,
2 int nrows, int ncols) {
3 ed_arg_t arg[NUM_THREADS];
4 pthread_t thread[NUM_THREADS];
5 int status, nslices, col0, i;
6 nslices=NUM_THREADS;
7 for (i=0; i < nslices; ++i) {
8 col0=i;
9 pack_arg(&arg[i], out_pixels, in_pixels, col0, nslices, nrows,
ncols);
10 pthread_create(&thread[i], NULL, edge_detect_thread, &arg[i]);
11 }
12 for (i=0; i < nslices; ++i) {
13 pthread_join(thread[i], (void *) &status);
14 }
15 return NULL;
16 }
```

Figure 9.5 A RAW data dependence error.

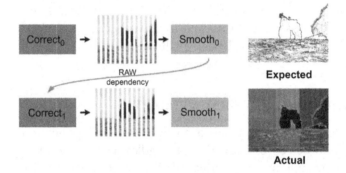

Figure 9.6 Visual of the RAW data dependency error introduced during attempt 1.

How does this work? Well not so well. I have introduced a functional error into the code. Diagnosis (Figure 9.5) shows that I have introduced a RAW data dependency. Basically there is a race condition, where $Smooth_0$ can read the image data before it has been written by the Correct function. You can see this error in Figure 9.6.

9.10 DATA PARALLEL—SECOND TRY

Let's try this again. The fix to this specific problem is to finish each function before starting next in order to prevent the race condition. What we will do is "join" the threads after each function before starting the subsequent function in order to alleviate this problem. The code below shows this. We create threads for the Correct, Smooth, and Detect functions in lines 3, 8, and 13, respectively. We add "join"

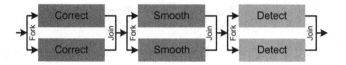

Figure 9.7 Join instructions added after each function fixes the race condition.

instructions at lines 5, 10, and 15. We can see how this works graphically in Figure 9.7.

```
1 for (i=0; i < nslices; ++i) {
2 pack_arg(&arg[i], out_pixels, in_pixels, i, nslices, nrows, ncols);
3 pthread_create(&thread[i], NULL, correct, &arg[i]);
4 }
5 for (i=0; i < nslices; ++i) pthread_join(thread[i], (void *) &status);
6 for (i=0; i < nslices; ++i) {
7 pack_arg(&arg[i], in_pixels, out_pixels, i, nslices, nrows, ncols);
8 pthread_create(&thread[i], NULL, smooth, &arg[i]);
9 }
10 for (i=0; i < nslices; ++i) pthread_join(thread[i], (void *)
&status);
11 for (i=0; i < nslices; ++i) {
12 pack_arg(&arg[i], out_pixels, in_pixels, i, nslices, nrows, ncols);
13 pthread_create(&thread[i], NULL, detect, &arg[i]);
14 }
15 for (i=0; i < nslices; ++i) pthread_join(thread[i], (void *)
&status);
```

This is now functionally correct. One thing to note: Interleaving columns probably is not good for data locality but this was easy to get working, so let's take the "make it work right, then make it work fast" approach for the moment.

9.11 TASK PARALLEL—THIRD TRY

The next strategy is to try to partition functions into a simple task pipeline. We can address the load balancing concern mentioned earlier by delaying the Smooth and Detect functions until enough pixels are ready. Figure 9.8 shows this pipelining approach.

The code for this is shown below. We create our queues in lines 3 and 5. Three threads are created for each function in the algorithm in line 7. We fill our queues in lines 10 and 11, and then join the threads back together in line 13.

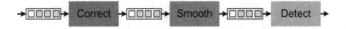

Figure 9.8 Pipelining architecture for the edge detect algorithm.

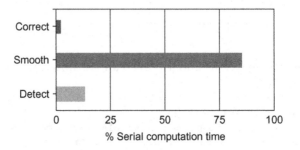

Figure 9.9 Unbalanced stages in the pipelining approach.

```
1 stage_f stage[3] = { correct, smooth, sobel};
2 queue_t *queue[4];
3 queue[0] = queue_create(capacity);
4 for (i=0; i < 3; ++i) {
5  queue[i + 1] = queue_create(capacity);
6  pack_arg(&arg[i], queue[i + 1], queue[i], nrows, ncols);
7  pthread_create(&thread[i], NULL, stage[i], &arg[i]);
8 }
9 while (*in_pixels) {
10  queue_add(queue[0], *in_pixels++);
11 } queue_add(queue[0], NULL);
12 for (i=0; i < 3; ++i) {
13 pthread_join(thread[i], &status);
14 }
```

The results are improved throughput but not latency. The throughput is limited by the longest stage ($1/85\% = 1.12\times$). This approach would be difficult to scale with number of cores. The latency is still the same, but like a pipeline, throughput improves. Remember that the stages are very imbalanced, so performance is not very good (Figure 9.9). We could consider doing data parallelism within the longest stage to better balance the stages. We can see a comparison of sequential and pipelined schedules in Figure 9.10.

9.12 EXPLORATION RESULTS

So far we have some interesting exploration results. We should go with the data decomposition approach. We should match the number of

Sequential schedule

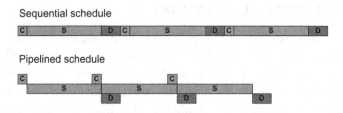

Pipelined schedule

Figure 9.10 Comparison of sequential and pipelined schedules.

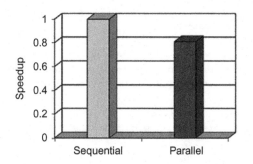

Figure 9.11 Slowdown in parallel processing indicates a potential cache locality problem.

threads to the number of cores, since the threads are compute intensive with few data dependencies that will block the threads. There are still some tuning opportunities that we can take advantage of. We have seen some interleaving concerns in one of our approaches and experienced some delay required for the pipelining design.

9.13 TUNING

We eventually want to identify and optimize performance issues. These could include thread stalls, excessive synchronization, and cache thrashing.

This is where we iterate and experiment. Vary the number of threads and number of cores. Look for ways to minimize locking. Try to separate threads from tasks in different ways to see the impact.

Analysis shows the results of this recent approach made performance worse that the sequential code (Figure 9.11)! Diagnosis shows false sharing between caches, a significant performance degradation.

9.14 DATA PARALLEL—THIRD TRY

Let's try a new strategy. Let's partition the application by contiguous slices of rows. This should help with data locality and potentially eliminate the false sharing problem as well. The code for this is shown below. We will refactor the code to process slices of rows for each thread for each function. We create the row slices for the Correct function in lines 1−4, then create the threads in line 5. We do a similar thing for the Smooth and Detect functions before joining them all back together again in line 26.

```
1 for (i = 0; i < nslices; ++i) {
2   row0 = i * srows;
3   row1 = (row0 + srows < nrows)? row0 + srows : nrows;
4   pack_arg(&arg[ i] , out_pixels, in_pixels, row0, row1, nrows, ncols);
5   pthread_create(&thread[ i] , NULL, correct_rows_thread, &arg[ i] );
6 }
7 for (i = 0; i < nslices; ++i) {
8   pthread_join(thread[ i] , (void *) &status);
9 }
10 for (i = 0; i < nslices; ++i) {
11   row0 = i * srows;
12   row1 = (row0 + srows < nrows)? row0 + srows : nrows;
13   pack_arg(&arg[ i] , in_pixels, out_pixels, row0, row1, nrows,
ncols);
14   pthread_create(&thread[ i] , NULL, smooth_rows_thread, &arg[ i] );
15 }
16 for (i = 0; i < nslices; ++i) {
17   pthread_join(thread[ i] , (void *) &status);
18 }
19 for (i = 0; i < nslices; ++i) {
20   row0 = i * srows;
21   row1 = (row0 + srows < nrows)? row0 + srows : nrows;
22   pack_arg(&arg[ i] , out_pixels, in_pixels, row0, row1, nrows,
ncols);
23   pthread_create(&thread[ i] , NULL, detect_rows_thread, &arg[ i] );
24 }
25 for (i = 0; i < nslices; ++i) {
26   pthread_join(thread[ i] , (void *) &status);
27 }
```

9.15 DATA PARALLEL—THIRD RESULTS

The results of this iteration are better. We have good localization of data and this also scales well. Data locality is important in multicore

Figure 9.12 Blocking and other cache optimizations can improve performance.

application. Traditional data layout optimization and loop transformation techniques apply to multicore:

- Minimize cache misses
- Maximize cache line usage
- Minimize the number of cores which touch a data item

Use the guidelines discussed earlier to achieve the best data locality for the application and significant performance results will be achieved. Use profiling and cache measurement tools to help you.

9.16 DATA PARALLEL—FOURTH TRY

We are now at a point where we can continue to make modifications to the application to improve cache performance. We can split rows into slices matching the L1 cache width of the device (example of this is blocking where the image can be decomposed into the appropriate block sizes as shown in Figure 9.12). We can process rows by slices for better data locality. In the end, additional data layout improvements are possible. Some of these could have been sequential optimizations so make sure you look for those opportunities first. It makes it easier when migrating to multicore, having already incorporated key optimizations into the sequential application.

9.17 DATA PARALLEL—WORK QUEUES

As an additional tuning strategy we can try using work queues (Figure 9.13). In this approach we attempt to separate the number of

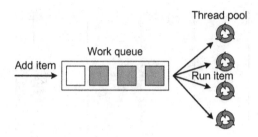

Figure 9.13 Work queues can help with performance and abstraction.

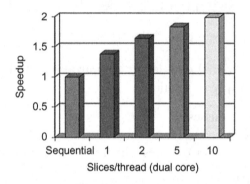

Figure 9.14 Track results to assess performance improvements.

tasks from the number of threads. This enables finer-grained tasks without extra thread overhead. Locking and condition variables which can cause extra complexity are hidden in work queue abstractions.

When we use this approach, the results get better as slices get smaller (Figure 9.14). The key is to tune empirically. In this example, we sacrificed some data locality—the work items are interleaved, but empirically, this is minor. The results are improved load balancing, some loss of data locality, but also easy to tune thread and work item granularity.

```
1 #define SLICES_PER_THREAD 5
2 nslices=NUM_THREADS * SLICES_PER_THREAD;
3 srows=nrows / nslices; if (nrows % nslices) ++srows;
4 crew=work_queue_create("Work Crew", nslices, NUM_THREADS);
5 for (i=0; i < nslices; ++i) {
6   r0=i * srows;
7   r1=(r0 + srows < nrows)? r0 + srows : nrows;
8   pack_arg(&arg[ i] , out_pixels, in_pixels, r0, r1, nrows, ncols);
9   work_queue_add_item(crew, edge_detect_rows, &arg[ i] );
10  } work_queue_empty(&crew);
```

Figure 9.15 Lag processing in the Correct/Smooth/Detect functions.

9.18 GOING TOO FAR?

Can we do even more? Probably. We can use task parallel learnings to compose three functions into one. We can do some more complex refactoring like lagging row processing to honor dependencies (Figure 9.15). This could lead to a three times reduction in thread creates and joins. This is possible with only minor duplicated computations at region edge. This modest performance improvement comes with increased coding complexity. See the code below to implement lag processing in this application.

This code is certainly more efficient but it is noticeably more complex. Is it necessary? Maybe or maybe not. Is the additional performance worth the complexity? This is a decision that must be made at some point. "Excessive optimization" can be harmful if the performance is not needed. Be careful with "premature optimization" and "excessive optimization."

```
1 void * edge_detect_rows (pixel_t out_pixels[], pixel_t in_pixels[],
2   int row0, int row1, int nrows, int ncols) {
3  int rc, rs, rd, rs_edge, rd_edge;
4  int nlines, scols, c0, c1, i;
5  pixel_t * corrected_pixels, * smoothed_pixels;
6  corrected_pixels = MEM_MALLOC (pixel_t, SMOOTH_SIDE * ncols);
7  smoothed_pixels = MEM_MALLOC (pixel_t, DETECT_SIDE * ncols);
8  // determine number of line splits
9  nlines = ncols / CACHE_LINESIZE;
10  scols = ncols / nlines;
11  if (ncols % nlines) ++scols;
12  for (i = 0; i < nlines; ++i) {
13   c0 = i * scols;
14   c1 = (c0 + scols < ncols)? c0 + scols : ncols;
15   log_debug1 ("row %d:%d col %d:%d\n", row0, row1, c0, c1);
16   for (rc = row0; rc < row1 + SMOOTH_EDGE + DETECT_EDGE; ++rc) {
17    if (rc < nrows) {
18     correct_row (corrected_pixels, in_pixels, rc % SMOOTH_SIDE, rc,
20      c0, c1, ncols);
21    }
22    rs = rc - SMOOTH_EDGE;
```

```
23    if (0 <= rs && rs < nrows) {
24     rs_edge = (rs < SMOOTH_EDGE || nrows - SMOOTH_EDGE <= rs) ? 1 : 0;
25     smooth_row(smoothed_pixels, corrected_pixels, rs %
       DETECT_SIDE,
26        rs_edge, rs % SMOOTH_SIDE, SMOOTH_SIDE, c0, c1, ncols);
27     }
28    rd = rs - DETECT_EDGE;
29    if (0 <= rd && rd < nrows) {
30     rd_edge = ((rd < DETECT_EDGE) ? -1 : 0) +
31           ((nrows - DETECT_EDGE <= rd) ? 1 : 0);
32     detect_row(out_pixels, smoothed_pixels, rd, rd_edge,
33        rd % DETECT_SIDE, DETECT_SIDE, c0, c1, ncols);
34 }}}
35 MEM_FREE(corrected_pixels);
36 MEM_FREE(smoothed_pixels);
37 return NULL;
38 }
```

10

Concurrency Abstractions

Writing code for multicore can be tedious and time-consuming. Here is an example. Below is the sequential code for a simple Dot Product:

```
#define SIZE 1000
Main() {
  double a[SIZE] , b[SIZE] ;
  // Compute a and b
  double sum = 0.0;
  for(int i = 0, i < SIZE; i++)
    sum + = a[i] * b[i] ;
  // use sum....
}
```

Now let's implement this same Dot Product using pthreads for a 4 core multicore processor. Here is the code below:

```
#include <iostream>
#include <pthread.h>
#define THREADS 4
#define SIZE 1000
using namespace std;
double a[SIZE] , b[SIZE] , sum;
pthread_mutex mutex_sum;
void *dotprod(void *arg) {
  int my_id = (int)arg;
  int my_first = my_id * SIZE/THREADS;
  int my_last = (my_id + 1) * SIZE/THREADS;
  double partial_sum = 0;
  for(int i = my_first; i < my_last && i < SIZE; i++)
    partial_sum + = a[i] * b[i];
  pthread_nmutex_lock(&mutex_sum);
  sum + = partial_sum;
pthread_mutex_unlock(&mutex_sum);
pthread_exit((void*)0);
}
int main(int argc, char *argv[]) {
// compute a and b...
pthread_attr_t attr;
pthread_t threads[THREADS] ;
```

Multicore Software Development Techniques. DOI: http://dx.doi.org/10.1016/B978-0-12-800958-1.00010-3

```
pthread_mutex_init(&mutex_sum, NULL);
pthread_attr_init(&attr);
pthread_attr_setdetachstate(&attr, PTHREAD_CREATE_JOINABLE);
sum = 0;
for(int i = 0; i < THREADS; i++)
pthread_create(&threads[i], &attr, dotprod, (void*)i);
  pthread__attr_destroy(&attr);
  int status;
  for(int i = 0, i < THREADS; i++)
    pthread_join(threads[i], (void**)&status);
  // use sum....
  pthread_mutex_destroy(&mutex_sum);
  pthread_exit(NULL);
}
```

As you can see, this implementation, although probably much faster on a multicore processor, is rather tedious and difficult to implement correctly. Lots of code is required to create and manage threads, protecting shared data etc. This do it yourself approach can definitely work but there are abstractions that can be used to make this process easier. That is what this section is about.

Multicore programming can be made easier using a concurrency abstraction. These include, but are not limited to:

• Language extensions
• Frameworks
• Libraries

There exist a wide variety of frameworks, language extensions, and libraries. Many of these are built upon the pthreads technology. pthreads is the API of POSIX-compliant operating systems like Linux used in many multicore applications.

Let's take a look at some of the different approaches to provide levels of multicore programming abstraction.

10.1 LANGUAGE EXTENSIONS EXAMPLE—OPENMP

OpenMP is an example of language extensions. Its actually an API that must be supported by the compiler. OpenMP uses multithreading as the method of parallelizing where a master thread forks a number of slave threads and the task is divided among these threads. The forked threads run concurrently on a runtime environment which allocates threads to different processor cores.

This requires application developer support. Each section of code that is a candidate to run in parallel must be marked with a preprocessor directive. This is an indicator to the compiler to insert instructions into the code to form threads before the indicated section is executed. Upon completion of the execution of the parallelized code, the threads join back into the master thread, and the application then continues in sequential mode again. This is shown in Figure 10.1.

Each thread executes the parallelized section of code independently. There exist various work-sharing constructs that can be used to divide a task among the threads so that each thread executes its allocated part of the code. Both task parallelism and data parallelism can be achieved this way. Figure 10.2 shows an example of how code can be instrumented to achieve this parallelism. The execution graph is shown in Figure 10.3.

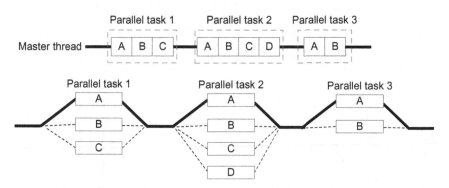

Figure 10.1 OpenMP mode of multicore parallel execution.

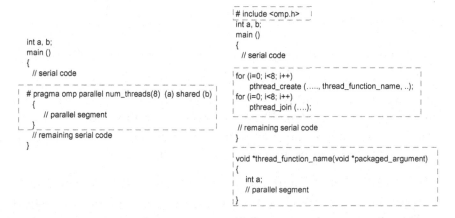

Figure 10.2 Instrumenting code to achieve parallelism in OpenMP. Original code is shown on the left, and the modified code is shown on the right.

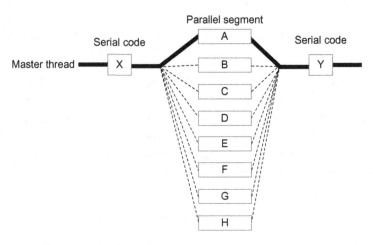

Figure 10.3 The execution flow for the example in Figure 10.2.

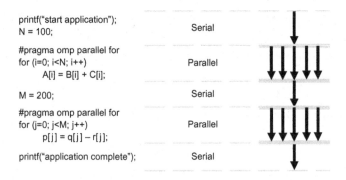

Figure 10.4 Using pragma's to turn a sequential piece of code (left) into a combination of serial and parallel execution sections (right).

Using basic OpenMP programming constructs can lead you towards realizing Amdahl's Law by parallelizing those parts of a program that the application developer has identified to be concurrent and leaving the serial portions unaffected (Figure 10.3).

OpenMP programs start with an initial master thread operating in a sequential region. When a parallel region is encountered (indicated by the compiler directive "#pragma omp parallel" in Figure 10.4) new threads called worker threads are created by the run time scheduler. These threads execute simultaneously on the block of parallel code. When the parallel region ends, the program waits for all threads to terminate (called a "join"), and then resumes its single-threaded execution for the next sequential region as shown in Figure 10.5.

The OpenMP specification support several important programming constructs:

1. Support of parallel regions
2. Worksharing across processing elements
3. Support of different data environments (shared, private, ...)
4. Support of synchronization concepts (barrier, flush, ...)
5. Runtime functions/environment variables

We will not go into the details of all of the APIs and programming constructs for OpenMP but there are a few items to keep in mind when using this approach:

Loops must have a canonical shape in order for OpenMP to parallelize it. Be careful using loops like this:

```
for (i = 0; i < max; i++) zero[i] = 0;
```

It is necessary for the OpenMP run-time system to determine loop iterations. Also, no premature exits from loops allowed (i.e., *break, return, exit, goto,* etc.).

The number of threads that OpenMP can create is defined by the OMP_NUM_THREADS environment variable. The developer should set this variable to the maximum number of threads you want OpenMP to use, which should be at least one per core/processor.

10.2 FRAMEWORK EXAMPLE—OPENCL

One of the challenges of multicore is the vendor centric approach, especially in heterogeneous multicore. Creating an application for heterogeneous parallel processing is a challenge because programming approaches for multicore CPUs and GPUs are quite different.

These limitations make it difficult for a developer to access the compute power of heterogeneous CPUs, GPUs, DSPs, and other types of processors from a single, multiplatform software code base.

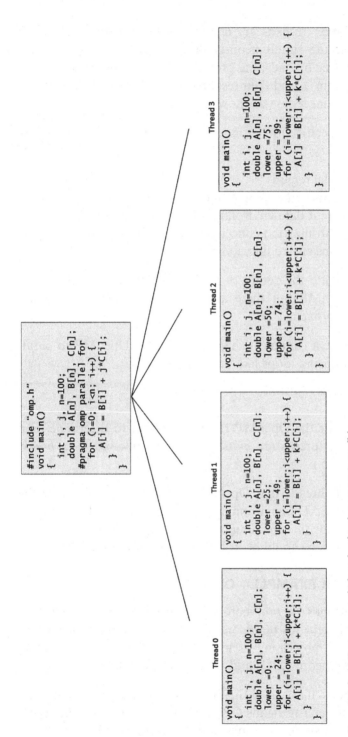

Figure 10.5 OpenMP can spawn multiple worker threads to process in parallel.

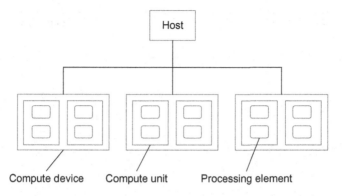

Figure 10.6 OpenCL model of host, compute device, compute unit, and processing element.

An OpenCL model is composed of a host which is connected to one or more devices. A device is divided into one or more compute units (CU). These CUs are divided into one or more processing elements (PEs). Computations on a device occur within the processing elements on that device (see Figure 10.6).

A device can be a CPU, GPU, or DSP, for example. A compute unit may be a core or multiprocessor. Processing elements are things that execute instructions together (e.g., SIMD-style).

An OpenCL application is designed as host software and device kernel software. The host software is implemented based on the programming models native to that host platform. The host software sends commands to the devices to perform computations. Each device executes these commands on the processing elements in the device.

OpenCL defines an execution model for parallel programming as shown in Figure 10.7.

We start with the assumption that an application needs access to system resources to perform some computation. The OpenCL execution model defines the interaction between the host application and one or more of the devices. OpenCL does this by establishing a context that encapsulates system resources into logical groupings (a container to hold compute resources for your system).

The context defined can be in terms of memory, programs, and queues as described in Figure 10.8

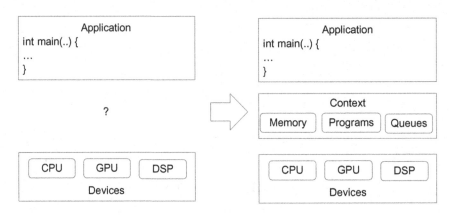

Figure 10.7 Execution model for OpenCL defines a context for encapsulation.

The state machine for the execution model can be described by the following flow (Figure 10.9):

1. Queued: The command is enqueued to a command-queue. A command will remain in the queue until it is flushed either explicitly.
2. Submitted: The command is flushed from the command-queue and submitted for execution on an OpenCL device. When the command is flushed from the command-queue, it will execute after any prerequisites for execution are met.
3. Ready: At this point, all prerequisites constraining execution of a command have been met. The command is placed in a device work-pool from which it is scheduled for execution.
4. Running: The command execution starts.
5. Ended: Execution of a command ends. When a kernel-enqueue command ends, all of the work-groups associated with that command have finished their execution.
6. Complete: The command and its child commands have finished execution.

The basic steps for creating an OpenCL program are as follows:

1. OpenCL Code
   a. Create the OpenCL code you want to run using OpenCL C based language;
2. Host Code
   a. Create your program (using C, for example);
   b. Create the data you want to process;

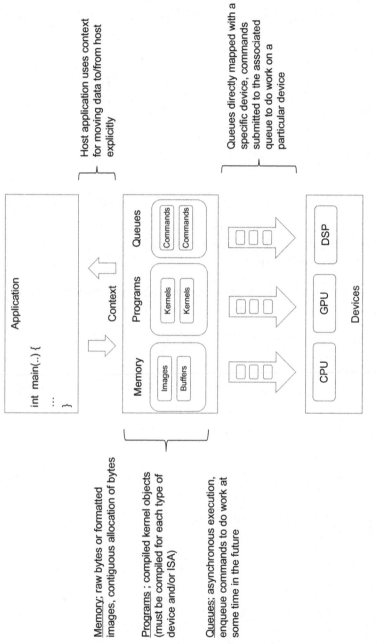

Memory; raw bytes or formatted images, contiguous allocation of bytes

Programs ; compiled kernel objects (must be compiled for each type of device and/or ISA)

Queues; asynchronous execution, enqueue commands to do work at some time in the future

Host application uses context for moving data to/from host explicitly

Queues directly mapped with a specific device, commands submitted to the associated queue to do work on a particular device

Figure 10.8 Details of OpenCL application context.

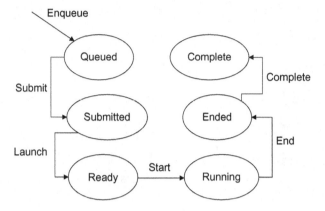

Figure 10.9 State machine for the execution model of OpenCL.

   c. Use the OpenCL API to transfer data to the devices;
   d. Use the OpenCL API to call executions;
   e. Retrieve any needed data.

OpenCL has a rich set of APIs to manage execution. A simple OpenCL program is shown below with comments;

```
private void test_program(object sender, EventArgs e)
{
  // initialize devices
  CLCalc.InitCL();
  // create required variables to be passed to OpenCL
  float[ ] a = new float[ ] { 1, 2, 3, 0.123f );
  float[ ] a = new float[ ] { 1, 2, 1, 2);
  // OpenCL source code, this string will be compiled by the OpenCL
compiler
  string s = @"
    kernel void
    sum (global float4 * x, global float4 * y)
    {
        x[0] = x[0] + y[0];
    }
  // compile the program
  CLCalc.Program.Compile(new string[ ] { s });
  // get a handle to the OpenCL function to call
  CLCalc.Program.Kernel sum = new CLCalc.Program.Kernel("sum");
  // copy variables x and y to OpenCL device memory
  CLCalc.Program.Variable varx = new CLCalc.Program.Variable(x);
  CLCalc.Program.Variable varx = new CLCalc.Program.Variable(y);
  // communicate arguments to OpenCL
  CLCalc.Program.Variable[ ] args = { varx, vary };
```

```
// define the number of work items
int[ ] max = new int[ ] { 1 };
// execute sum code with arguments specified
sum.Execute(args, max);
// read x variable from video memory
varx.ReadFromDeviceTo(x);
}
```

10.3 LIBRARIES EXAMPLE—THREAD BUILDING LIBRARIES

Parallel libraries will help reduce programmer development time as well as promote code portability and reuse, and, when developed properly, improve code performance. There are several examples of these libraries:

* Native thread libraries
* Java Concurrency
* Python thread library
* Parallel Libraries already threaded and/or thread-safe
* Intel Threading Building Blocks

Intel Thread Building Blocks (TBB) is a C++ template library for developing multicore software. The library includes data structures and algorithms that help a developer avoid some of the complexity of using lower-level APIs. This complexity exists in the form of complications in creating, synchronizing, and terminating threads.

TBB abstracts access to multiple cores/processors by providing operations to be treated as "tasks," which can be allocated to individual cores dynamically. TBB are implemented to make efficient use of cache. TBB provides a variety of templates for common parallel programming patterns, such as nested parallelism constructs, software loops, and software pipelining.

TBB support many basic multicore programming concepts such as:

* Basic multicore algorithms
* Some advanced multicore concepts
* Containers
* Memory allocation
* Mutual exclusion
* Atomic operations
* Timing
* Task scheduling

TBB uses a concept called "work stealing" for load balancing threads between cores. This approach assumes a queue of work items (e.g., threads) to execute. When a processor runs out of work, it looks at the queues of other processors and "steals" their work items.

```
#include "tbb/tbb.h"
#include <cstdio>
using namespace tbb;
class hello_world
{
    const char* id;
    public:
            hello_world(const char* s) : id(s) { }
            void operator ( ) ( ) const
            {
            printf("hello world from task %s\n",id);
            }
};
int main ( )
{
    task_group tg;
    tg.run(hello_world("1")); // spawn task 1
    tg.run(hello_world("2")); // spawn task 2
    tg.wait( ); // wait for tasks to complete
}
```

TBB has a comprehensive library of routines to help in the areas listed above. TBB is open source; you can download it here (http://threadingbuildingblocks.org/).

10.4 THREAD SAFETY

While we are on the topic of threads, we need to understand what it means to have a "thread-safe" code.

A segment of code is referred to as "thread-safe" if it manipulates shared data structures in such as way that guarantees safe execution by multiple threads at the same time. This means that a thread-safe piece of code must take specific precautions to prevent multiple threads from accessing a shared resource. These precautions include:

- all accesses to the shared data structure must have no effect on the resource

- all accesses to the shared data structure are idempotent, in other words, the order of operations does not affect the outcome
- only one access to the shared data structure is allowed at a time

Other precautions must be observed. For example, all functions called from a thread (without external synchronization) must also be thread-safe. This means that the function must always produce correct results when called repeatedly from multiple concurrent threads in the multicore system.

Code that is "unsafe" includes code:

- That fails to protect all shared variables and resources
- That depends on persistent state across invocations
- That returns a pointer static variable(s)
- That calls thread-unsafe functions

There are several ways to make code thread-safe.

- Use mutexes to protect shared data. Keep in mind that synchronization operations will slow down code use—make sure you use these wisely.
- Make objects or functions immutable. This means that the object of function state cannot be changed after the object is created. There are a couple ways to make objects immmutable (e.g., avoiding shared state);
  - Make your code reentrant. This involves writing code in such a way that it can be partially executed by a thread, reexecuted by the same thread or simultaneously executed by another thread and still correctly complete the original execution. In order to accomplish this, state information must be saved in variables local to each thread execution (usually on a stack) instead of in static or global variables or other nonlocal state. If nonlocal state is required, then all nonlocal state must be accessed through atomic operations. Data-structures must also be reentrant.
  - Thread-local storage. With this approach, variables are localized in such a way that each thread has its own private copy of the variables. These variables will retain their values across subroutine and other code boundaries. They are considered thread-safe since they are local to each thread. If the code which accesses these variables are executed simultaneously by another thread, correct operation will be ensured.

- Do not use pointers to static variables. This can be fixed by rewriting code so the caller passes a pointer to a structure. This will require changes in the caller and callee. A "lock and copy" approach can also be used which requires relatively simple changes in the caller and none in the callee. The called must be responsible for freeing memory in this approach.
- Do not call thread-unsafe functions. Calling one thread-unsafe function makes the entire function that calls it thread-unsafe. This can be solved by modifying the function so it calls only thread-safe functions. Check your libraries carefully. All functions in the Standard C Library are thread-safe (e.g., malloc, free, printf, scanf, etc.).
- Use a thread safe "wrapper." Using this approach, a new thread-safe class has objects of original class as fields, and the wrapper class provides methods to access original class object.

10.5 MESSAGE PASSING MULTICORE MODELS—MPI AND MCAPI

In multicore processors, as well as embedded systems in general, inter-process communication consists of synchronization as well as movement of data from one process's address space to another's. As shown in Figure 10.10, a sender has data to send, it determines whether it is ok to send this data, gets a confirmation, and then sends the data to one or more places/processors.

Message-passing specifications are available that extend existing message-passing models. These are not a language or compiler specification and are not a specific implementation or product. Two popular message passing models for multicore are Message Passing Interface (MPI) and Multicore Communications API (MCAPI).

MPI is a language-independent message passing and communications protocol for programming multicore and other parallel computers.

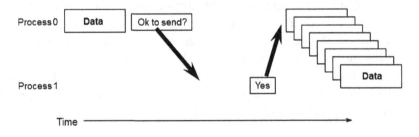

Figure 10.10 Message passing model.

Point-to-point and collective communication models are supported with the MPI API.

A simple "hello world" MPI program is shown below. This "C" MPI program will send a "hello" message to each processor, perform a simple computation, and then return the results to the main process, and print the messages. The output from this program will be:

0: There are 2 processors
0: Hello World! Processor 1 now on line

```c
/*
   "Hello World" MPI Program
 */
#include <mpi.h>
#include <stdio.h>
#include <string.h>

#define BUFSIZE 256
#define TAG 0

int main(int argc, char *argv[])
{
        char id_string[32];
        char buff[BUFSIZE];
        int num_processors;
        int my_id;
        int i;

        MPI_Status status;

        /* Start by initializing all processors */
        MPI_Init(&argc, &argv);

        /* find out how many processors are participating in the
computation */
        MPI_Comm_size(MPI_COMM_WORLD, &num_processors);

        /* find out what processor I am */
        MPI_Comm_rank(MPI_COMM_WORLD, &my_id);

        /* all programs are now running, use the rank to determine the
roles of the programs in the system, rank 0 can be the master processor */
        if (my_id == 0)
        {
            printf("%d: there are %d processors\n", my_id,
num_processors);
            for (i = 1; i < num_processors; i++)
            {
                sprintf(buff, "Hello World %d!", i);
                MPI_Send(buff, BUFSIZE, MPI_CHAR, i, TAG,
MPI_COMM_WORLD);
```

```
        }
        for(i = 1; i < num_processors; i++)
        {
              MPI_Recv(buff, BUFSIZE, MPI_CHAR, i, TAG,
MPI_COMM_WORLD, &stat);
              printf("%d: %s\n", my_id, buff);
        }
    }
    else
    {
        /* receive from rank 0: */
        MPI_Recv(buff, BUFSIZE, MPI_CHAR, 0, TAG, MPI_COMM_WORLD,
&stat);
        sprintf(idstr, "Processor %d ", my_id);
        strncat(buff, id_string, BUFSIZE-1);
        strncat(buff, "now on line", BUFSIZE-1);

        /* send information to processor with rank 0: */
        MPI_Send(buff, BUFSIZE, MPI_CHAR, 0, TAG,
MPI_COMM_WORLD);
    }

    /* MPI Finalize is a synchronization point for MPI programs */
    MPI_Finalize();
    return 0;
}
```

The Multicore Communications API (MCAPI) specification defines an API as well as a semantic for communication and synchronization between processing cores primarily focused on embedded systems (Figure 10.11), and similar to a socket programming model for networking.

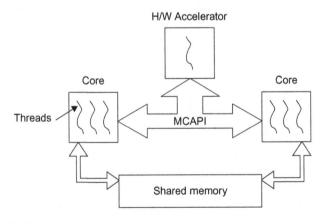

Figure 10.11 MCAPI communication model.

The basic MCAPI model defines each core as an individual node in the system. When a node needs to communicate with another node, it specifies an endpoint for sending or receiving data.

MCAPI defines three fundamental communications types. These are:

1. Messages—connectionless datagrams (most flexible, useful when senders and receivers are dynamically changing and communicate infrequently, and commonly used for synchronization and initialization).
    a. Packet channels—connection-oriented, unidirectional, FIFO packet streams.
    b. Scalar channels—connection-oriented single word unidirectional, FIFO packet streams.

Unlike other communication protocols, MCAPI does not require a full TCP/IP stack to exchange data. It was designed to be light weight for a variety of embedded systems applications where scarce resources are the norm.

The MCAPI model represents cores in a multicore systems as "nodes" (Figure 10.12). When one node needs to communicate with another node an "endpoint" is created. This is similar to a TCP/IP socket. APIs are then used to send and receive data to and from the

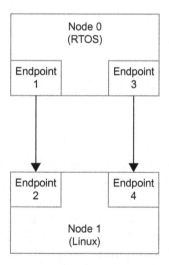

Figure 10.12 MCAPI endpoint configuration.

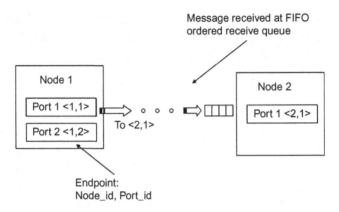

Figure 10.13 Endpoint communication model in MCAPI.

endpoint, using the low level drivers to do the work. In Figure 10.13, Node 0 is running and RTOS, and Node 1 is running Linux. Two communication channels are established. Endpoints 1 and 2 are established to send and receive one stream of data. Endpoints 3 and 4 are similarly created to send and receive other data independently. This is an interrupt-driven approach to sending/receiving data which ensures that each data buffer transmitted will be received in the proper order (Figure 10.13).

To manage endpoint communications, MCAPI APIs can be used. An example is shown below:

```
void mcapi_msg_send(
        MCAPI_IN mcapi_endpoint_t send_endpoint,
        MCAPI_IN mcapi_endpoint_t receive_endpoint,
        MCAPI_IN void* buffer,
        MCAPI_IN size_t buffer_size,
        MCAPI_IN mcapi_priority_t priority,
        MCAPI_OUT mcapi_status_t* mcapi_status
    );
```

This API can be used to send a message between the two endpoints (send_endpoint and receive_endpoint) in Figure 10.14. This API acts as a blocking call and returns when the buffer is available to be reused by the application (a nonblocking variant is also defined in the MCAPI specification). Endpoint messages are placed in the defined "buffer" with size "buffer_size" and priority "priority." The pointer mcapi_status points to the location where the result of the call will be placed.

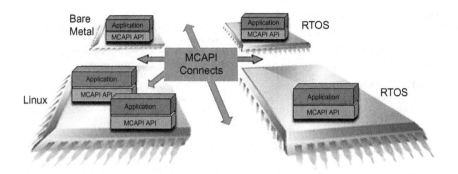

Figure 10.14 An example multicore platform requiring MCAPI.

A simple example of a program to set up these endpoints is shown below:

```
int main () {
...
for (t = 0; t < NUM_THREADS; t++) {
    app = pthread_create( .. );
}
  for (t = 0; t < NUM_THREADS; t++) {
    pthread_join( .. );
    }
}
void* run_thread (void *t) {
...
  mcapi_initialize( .. );
  if (task_id == 1) {
  receive_endpoint =
  mcapi_create_endpoint (P_NUM, ..);
  mcapi_msg_recv(receive_endpoiint, ..);
  mcapi_msg_recv(receive_endpoint, ..);
}
else {
send_endpoint = mcapi_create_endpoint
          (P_NUM, ..);
recv_endpt = mcapi_get_endpoint
          (1, P_NUM, ..);
mcapi_msg_send(send_endpoint, receive_endpoint, ..);
}
mcapi_finalize( .. );
return NULL;
}
```

MCAPI APIs can be layered on top of existing communication pro-tocols or scaled from higher end applications to lower end applications

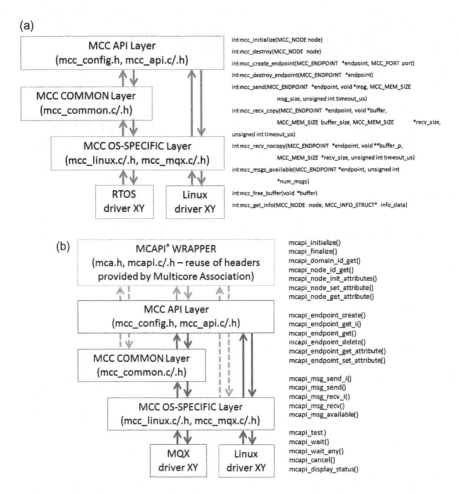

Figure 10.15 (a) Existing API for a heterogeneous multicore application. (b) MCAPI wrapper on top of existing API to allow platform portability and scalability.

easily. Figure X shows a system designed for a platform with Linux running on an ARM Cortex®-A5 and an RTOS running on ARM® Cortex®-M4 core. This application should be designed to allow portability to other platforms as necessary.

This example system implements an API containing functions for message sending/receiving between endpoints, with both blocking and nonblocking options (Figure 10.14). Shared RAM, intercore interrupts and hardware semaphores are utilized in this design. All resources are statically configured at the compile time. An MCAPI API is flexible enough to be layered on top of the existing API to provide this platform portability (Figure 10.15).

10.6 LANGUAGE SUPPORT

Languages have changed to support multicore and it is worth mentioning this here. One in particular is C++11. C++11 is a core language change to support the challenges of the day, in this case multicore programming.

C++11 is a backwardly compatible upgrade to the C++ language. There are some new multithreading facilities in C++11, specifically related to software design and deployment on multicore platforms. These include support for threads, locking, and condition variables.

For example, remember that matrix multiply we discussed earlier. The "naïve" approach we started with is shown again below:

```
//
// matrix multiple, naïve version
//
for (int i = 0; i < N; i++)
{
    for (int j = 0; j < N; j++)
    {
        C[i][j] = 0.0;
        for (int k = 0; k < N; k++)
            C[i][j] += (A[i][k] * B[k][j]);
    }
}
```

C++11 uses a fork/join model similar to pthreads. This function can be implemented in C++11 as shown below:

```
1. int rows = N/numthreads;
2. int extra = N % numthreads;
3. int start = 0; // each thread does [start..end)
4. int end = rows;
5. auto code = [N, &C, &A, &B] (int start, int end) -> void
6. {
7. for (int i = start; i < end; i++)
8.    for (int j = 0; j < N; j++)
9.    {
10.       C[i][j] = 0.0;
11.       for (int k = 0; k < N; k++)
12.       C[i][j] += (A[i][k] * B[k][j]);
13.    }
14. };
15. vector<thread> workers;
16. for (int t = 1; t <= numthreads; t++)
```

```
17. {
18. if (t == numthreads) // last thread does extra rows:
19.   end += extra;
20.   workers.push_back( thread(code, start, end));
21.   start = end;
22.   end = start + rows;
23. }
24. for (std::thread& t : threads) // new range-based for:
25.   t.join();
```

In this code snippet, std::vector (line 15) is a sequence container that encapsulates dynamic size arrays.

Line 5 uses the "auto" function...if the compiler can infer the type of a variable at the point of declaration, instead of putting in the variable type, you can just use auto.

Line 20 uses the "threads.push_back" function which is an operator that appends the given element (in this case the thread(code) to the end of the container.

The "join" in line 26 implies that the function returns when the thread execution has completed. This synchronizes the moment this function returns with the completion of all the operations in the thread and blocks the execution of the thread that calls this function until the function called on construction returns.

So as you can see, there are language facilities being added to popular languages like C++ to support multicore computations. With the growing popularity of multicore, this trend will continue.

ADDITIONAL READING

Multicore Programming Practices, Multicore Association (http://www.multicore-association.org/).

Multicore Communication API, Multicore Association (http://www.multicore-association.org/).

OpenCL Specification, Khronos Group, (https://www.khronos.org/opencl/).

OpenMP Specification, OpenMP Group, (http://openmp.org/wp/).

MATRIX MULTIPLY — NAÏVE VERSION (NOT CACHE FRIENDLY)

```
1  /* mm.c */
2
3  //
4  // My Matrix Multiplication app
5  //
6  // Uses standard triply-nested loop, not cache-friendly.
7  //
8
9  // Usage:
10 //   mm[-?] [-n MatrixSize] [-t NumThreads]
11 //
12 #define LINUX
13 // #define WINDOWS
14
15 #include   <stdio.h>
16 #include   <stdlib.h>
17 #include   <string.h>
18 #include   <math.h>
19 #include   <time.h>
20
21 #ifdef LINUX
22 #include <sys/time.h>
23 #endif
24
25 #include "pthread.h"
26
27
28 //
29 // Function prototypes:
30 //
31 double **MatrixMultiply(double** A, double** B, int N, int numthreads);
32 void   _SequentialMM(double** C, double** A, double** B, int N);
33 void   _ParallelMM(double** C, double** A, double** B, int N, int
            numthreads);
34
35 void CreateAndFillMatrices(int N, double*** A, double*** B, double*
            TL, double* TR, double* BL, double* BR);
36 void CheckResults(int N, double** C, double TL, double TR, double BL,
            double BR);
```

```
37  void ProcessCmdLineArgs(int argc, char* argv[]);
38
39  double **New2dMatrix(int ROWS, int COLS);
40  void     Delete2dMatrix(double **matrix);
41
42  double  my_clock();
43  #define  Min(a,b) ((a)<(b)?(a):(b))
44
45
46  //
47  // Globals:
48  //
49  int _matrixSize;
50  int _numThreads;
51
52  //
53  // main:
54  //
55
56  int main(int argc, char *argv[])
57  {
58    double  startTime, stopTime, time;
59    double **A, **B, **C, TL, TR, BL, BR;
60
61    //
62    // Set defaults, process environment & cmd-line args:
63    //
64    _matrixSize = 512;
65    _numThreads = 1;    // pthread_num_processors_np();
66
67    ProcessCmdLineArgs(argc, argv);
68
69    printf("** My Matrix Multiply Application **\n\n");
70    printf("   Matrix size: %d x %d\n", _matrixSize, _matrixSize);
71    printf("   Num threads: %d\n", _numThreads);
72    printf("\n");
73    printf("** Running...\n\n");
74
75    //
76    // Create and fill the matrices to multiply:
77    //
78    CreateAndFillMatrices(_matrixSize, &A, &B, &TL, &TR, &BL, &BR);
79
80    //
81    // Start clock and multiply:
82    //
83    startTime = my_clock();
84
85    C = MatrixMultiply(A, B, _matrixSize, _numThreads);
86
87    stopTime = my_clock();
```

```
 88    time = stopTime - startTime;
 89
 90    //
 91    // Done, check results and output timing:
 92    //
 93    CheckResults(_matrixSize, C, TL, TR, BL, BR);
 94
 95    printf("** Success! Time: %4.2f secs\n", time);
 96    printf("** Execution complete **\n");
 97    printf("\n\n");
 98
 99    //
100    // cleanup:
101    //
102    Delete2dMatrix(A);
103    Delete2dMatrix(B);
104    Delete2dMatrix(C);
105
106    pthread_exit(NULL); // aka return:
107 }
108 //
109 // MatrixMultiply:
110 //
111 // Computes and returns C = A * B, where matrices are NxN.
112 //
113 // NOTE: this is the naive implementation of MM, which multiplies rows by
114 // columns, and doesn't take into account the memory hierarchy.
115 //
116 double** MatrixMultiply(double** A, double** B, int N, int numthreads)
117 {
118    double** C;
119    C = New2dMatrix(N, N);
120    if (numthreads <= 1) // sequential implementation:
121    {
122      _SequentialMM(C, A, B, N);
123    }
124    else // parallel implementation:
125    {
126      _ParallelMM(C, A, B, N, numthreads);
127    }
128    return C;
129 }
130
131
132 //
133 // Sequential:
134 //
135 void _SequentialMM(double** C, double** A, double** B, int N)
136 {
137    int i, j, k;
138    // initialize target matrix elements to 0:
```

```
139    for (i = 0; i < N; i++)
140        for (j = 0; j < N; j++)
141            C[i][j] = 0.0;
142    // now multiply: C = A * B
143    for (i = 0; i < N; i++)
144      for (j = 0; j < N; j++)
145        for (k = 0; k < N; k++)
146          C[i][j] += (A[i][k] * B[k][j]);
147 }
148
149 //
150 // Parallel:
151 //
152 typedef struct ThreadArgs
153 {
154   double**  A;
155   double**  B;
156   double**  C;
157   int       rstart;
158   int       rend;
159   int       N;
160 } ThreadArgs;
161
162 void _ParallelMM(double** C, double** A, double** B, int N, int numthreads)
163 {
164   //
165   // TODO: create 2 threads and split workload between them...
166   //
167
168   int i, j, k;
169
170   // initialize target matrix elements to 0:
171   for (i = 0; i < N; i++)
172     for (j = 0; j < N; j++)
173       C[i][j] = 0.0;
174
175   // now multiply: C = A * B
176   for (i = 0; i < N; i++)
177     for (j = 0; j < N; j++)
178       for (k = 0; k < N; k++)
179         C[i][j] += (A[i][k] * B[k][j]);
180 }
181
182
183 //
184 // CreateAndFillMatrices: fills A and B with predefined values, and then
185 // set TL, TR, BL and BR to the expected top-left, top-right, bottom-left
186 // and bottom-right values after the multiply.
187 //
188
```

```
189  void CreateAndFillMatrices(int N, double*** A, double*** B, double* TL,
       double* TR, double* BL, double* BR)
190  {
191    double **a;
192    double **b;
193    double    dN;
194    int       r, c;
195
196    a = New2dMatrix(N, N);
197    b = New2dMatrix(N, N);
198  //
199    // A looks like:
200    //  1 1 1 1 ... 1
201    //  2 2 2 2 ... 2
202    //  . . . . ... .
203    //  . . . . ... .
204    //  N N N N ... N
205    //
206    for (r = 0; r < N /* rows*/; r++)
207      for (c = 0; c < N /* cols*/; c++)
208        a[r][c] = r + 1;
209
210    //
211    // B looks like:
212    //  1 2 3 4 ... N
213    //  1 2 3 4 ... N
214    //  . . . . ... .
215    //  . . . . ... .
216    //  1 2 3 4 ... N
217    //
218    for (r = 0; r < N /* rows*/; r++)
219      for (c = 0; c < N /* cols*/; c++)
220        b[r][c] = c + 1;
221
222    //
223    // expected values:
224    //
225    dN = N;  // use double to overflow errors with large N:
226
227    *TL = dN;          // C[0,0]    == Sum(1..1)
228    *TR = dN* dN;      // C[0,N-1]  == Sum(N..N)
229    *BL = dN* dN;      // C[N-1, 0] == Sum(N..N)
230    *BR = dN* dN* dN;  // C[N-1, N-1] == SUM(N^2..N^2)
231
232    // return matrices back to caller:
233    *A = a;
234    *B = b;
235  }
```

```
236
237
238  //
239  // Checks the results against some expected results:
240  //
241  void CheckResults(int N, double** C, double TL, double TR, double BL,
         double BR)
242  {
243    int b1, b2, b3, b4;
244
245    b1 = ( fabs(C[0][0]     - TL) < 0.0000001 );
246    b2 = ( fabs(C[0][N-1]   - TR) < 0.0000001 );
247    b3 = ( fabs(C[N-1][0]   - BL) < 0.0000001 );
248    b4 = ( fabs(C[N-1][N-1] - BR) < 0.0000001 );
249
250    if (!b1 || !b2 || !b3 || !b4)
251    {
252      printf("** ERROR: matrix multiply yielded incorrect results\n\n");
253      exit(0);
254    }
255  }
256
257
258  //
259  // processCmdLineArgs:
260  //
261  void ProcessCmdLineArgs(int argc, char* argv[])
262  {
263    int i;
264    for (i = 1; i < argc; i++)
265    {
266
267      if (strcmp(argv[i], "-?") == 0)  // help:
268      {
269        printf("**Usage: mm [-?] [-n MatrixSize] [-t NumThreads]\n\n");
270        exit(0);
271      }
272      else if ((strcmp(argv[i], "-n") == 0) && (i+1 < argc))  // matrix size:
273      {
274        i++;
275        _matrixSize = atoi(argv[i]);
276      }
277      else if ((strcmp(argv[i], "-t") == 0) && (i+1 < argc))  // matrix size:
278      {
279        i++;
280        _numThreads = atoi(argv[i]);
281      }
282      else  // error: unknown arg
```

```
283      {
284          printf("**Unknown argument: '%s'\n", argv[i] );
285          printf("**Usage: mm[-?] [-n MatrixSize] [-t NumThreads]\n\n");
286          exit(0);
287      }
288
289    } //for
290  }
291  //
292
293  // Matrix allocation functions:
294  //
295
296  //
297  // New2dMatrix: allocates a 2D matrix of size ROWSxCOLS, which is really
298  // a 1D array of row pointers into a large, contiguous block of 1D memory.
299  // For example, in ASCII art, here's a 3x5 array:
300  //
301  //              ------------------------------
302  //              | | | | | | | | | | | | | | | |
303  //              ------------------------------
304  //                ^          ^          ^
305  //                |          |          |
306  //  ---           |          |          |
307  //  |-----------             |          |
308  //  ---                      |          |
309  //  |---------------------              |
310  //  ---                                 |
311  //  |-----------------------------------
312  //  ---
313  //
314  // Much more efficient for caching, if using MPI to send messages, etc.
315  //
316  double **New2dMatrix(int ROWS, int COLS)
317  {
318    double **matrix;
319    double *elements;
320    int      r;
321
322    //
323    // for efficiency of both allocation and transmission, we allocate the
324    // matrix as 1 large chunk of memory, then set the row pointers into
325    // this chunk:
326    //
327    matrix = (double **) malloc(ROWS * sizeof(double*));
328    elements = (double *) malloc(ROWS * COLS * sizeof(double));
329
330    for (r = 0; r < ROWS; r++)
```

```
331    matrix[r] = &elements[r * COLS] ;
332    return matrix;
333 }
334
335
336 //
337 // Delete2dMatrix: frees memory associated with 2D matrix allocated by
338 // New2dMatrix.
339 //
340 void Delete2dMatrix(double **matrix)
341 {
342    free(matrix[0] );
343    free(matrix);
344 }
345
346
347 //
348 // my_clock: clock function for Windows and Linux, returning time in secs
349 //
350 double my_clock()
351 {
352 #ifdef WINDOWS
353    return ((double) clock()) / CLOCKS_PER_SEC;
354 #endif
355
356 #ifdef LINUX
357    struct timeval t;
358
359    gettimeofday(&t, NULL);
360
361    return (1.0e-6 * t.tv_usec) + t.tv_sec;
362 #endif
363 }
```

MATRIX MULTIPLY—CACHE FRIENDLY VERSION

```
 1 /* mm-cache.c */
 2
 3 //
 4 // Cache-friendly Matrix Multiplication app
 5 //
 6 // Multiplies in a smarter way, taking memory hierarchy into account.
 7 // The result is a much more cache-friendly app, and more efficient.
 8 // For details, see
 9 // http://www.cs.rochester.edu/~sandhya/csc252/lectures/
   lecture-memopt.pdf
10 //
```

```
11  // Usage:
12  //   mm-cache[-?] [-n MatrixSize] [-b BlockSize] [-t NumThreads]
13  //
14
15  #define LINUX
16  // #define WINDOWS
17
18  #include <stdio.h>
19  #include <stdlib.h>
20  #include <string.h>
21  #include <math.h>
22  #include <time.h>
23
24  #ifdef LINUX
25  #include <sys/time.h>
26  #endif
27
28  #include "pthread.h"
29
30
31  //
32  // Function prototypes:
33  //
34  double **MatrixMultiply(double** A, double** B, int N, int BS, int
    numthreads);
35  void    _SequentialMM(double** C, double** A, double** B, int N, int BS);
36  void    _ParallelMM(double** C, double** A, double** B, int N, int BS,
               int numthreads);
37  void    *_DoParallelMM(void *args);
38
39  void CreateAndFillMatrices(int N, double*** A, double*** B, double*
    TL, double* TR, double* BL, double* BR);
40  void CheckResults(int N, double** C, double TL, double TR, double BL,
           double BR);
41  void ProcessCmdLineArgs(int argc, char* argv[]);
42
43  double **New2dMatrix(int ROWS, int COLS);
44  void    Delete2dMatrix(double **matrix);
45
46  double  my_clock();
47
48  #define Min(a,b) ((a)<(b)?(a):(b))
49
50
51  //
52  // Globals:
53  //
54  int _matrixSize;
55  int _numThreads;
```

```
56  int _blockSize;
57  int _setMatrixSize;
58  int _setBlockSize;
59
60
61  //
62  // main:
63  //
64  int main(int argc, char * argv[])
65  {
66    double  startTime, stopTime, time;
67    double **A, **B, **C, TL, TR, BL, BR;
68
69    //
70    // Set defaults, process environment & cmd-line args:
71    //
72    _matrixSize = 512;
73    _numThreads = 1;        // pthread_num_processors_np();
74    _blockSize = _matrixSize;
75    _setMatrixSize = 0;     // false:
76    _setBlockSize = 0;      // false:
77
78    ProcessCmdLineArgs(argc, argv);
79
80    // if the user set the matrix size but did not set the block size,
81    // then no blocking of the matrix should occur -- so set the block
82    // size == matrix size:
83    if (_setMatrixSize && !_setBlockSize)
84      _blockSize = _matrixSize;
85
86    printf("** Cache-friendly Matrix Multiply Application **\n\n");
87    printf("  Matrix size: %d x %d\n", _matrixSize, _matrixSize);
88    printf("  Num threads: %d\n", _numThreads);
89    printf("  Block size:  %d\n", _blockSize);
90    printf("\n");
91    printf("** Running...\n\n");
92
93    //
94    // Create and fill the matrices to multiply:
95    //
96    CreateAndFillMatrices(_matrixSize, &A, &B, &TL, &TR, &BL, &BR);
97
98    //
99    // Start clock and multiply:
100   //
101   startTime = my_clock();
102
103   C = MatrixMultiply(A, B, _matrixSize, _blockSize, _numThreads);
104
105   stopTime = my_clock();
```

```
106    time = stopTime - startTime;
107
108    //
109    // Done, check results and output timing:
110    //
111    CheckResults(_matrixSize, C, TL, TR, BL, BR);
112
113    printf("\n");
114    printf("** Success! Time: %4.2f secs\n", time);
115    printf("** Execution complete **\n");
116    printf("\n\n");
117
118    //
119    // cleanup:
120    //
121    Delete2dMatrix(A);
122    Delete2dMatrix(B);
123    Delete2dMatrix(C);
124
125    pthread_exit(NULL); // aka return:
126 }
127
128
129 //
130 // MatrixMultiply:
131 //
132 // Computes and returns C = A * B, where matrices are NxN and
133 // BS = blocksize for chunking.
134 //
135 // NOTE: if BS == N, then we aren't blocking at all, but perf still
136 // greatly improved due to loop interchange (and thus effectiveness
137 // of cache).
138 //
139 // Reference: "Writing Cache Friendly Code", U. of Rochester,
140 // http://www.cs.rochester.edu/~sandhya/csc252/lectures/
            lecture-memopt.pdf
141 //
142 double** MatrixMultiply(double** A, double** B, int N, int BS, int
      numthreads)
143 {
144    double** C;
145
146    C = New2dMatrix(N, N);
147
148    if (numthreads <= 1)  // sequential implementation:
149    {
150       _SequentialMM(C, A, B, N, BS);
151    }
152    else  // parallel implementation:
```

```
153   {
154      _ParallelMM(C, A, B, N, BS, numthreads);
155   }
156
157    return C;
158 }
159
160 //
161 // Sequential:
162 //
163 void _SequentialMM(double** C, double** A, double** B, int N, int BS)
164 {
165    int i, j, k;
166
167    if (BS < N) // then blocking is needed:
168    {
169
170        int jj, kk, jjEND, kkEND;
171
172        // for each block...
173        for (jj=0; jj<N; jj+=BS)
174        {
175          jjEND = Min(jj+BS, N);
176
177          // initialize:
178          for (i=0; i<N; i++)
179            for (j=jj; j < jjEND; j++)
180              C[i][j] = 0.0;
181
182          // block multiply:
183          for (kk=0; kk<N; kk+=BS)
184          {
185            kkEND = Min(kk+BS, N);
186
187            for (i=0; i<N; i++)
188              for (k=kk; k < kkEND; k++)
189                for (j=jj; j < jjEND; j++)
190                  C[i][j] += (A[i][k] * B[k][j] );
191          }
192        }
193
194    }
195    else // no blocking, just interchange inner-most j and k loops:
196    {
197
198        // initialize:
199        for (i = 0; i < N; i++)
200          for (j = 0; j < N; j++)
201            C[i][j] = 0.0;
202
```

```
203        // multiply:
204        for (i = 0; i < N; i++)
205          for (k = 0; k < N; k++)
206            for (j = 0; j < N; j++)
207              C[i][j] += (A[i][k] * B[k][j]);
208
209   }
210 }
211 //
212 // Parallel:
213 //
214 typedef struct ThreadArgs
215 {
216   double** A;
217   double** B;
218   double** C;
219   int      rstart;
220   int      rend;
221   int      N;
222   int      BS;
223 } ThreadArgs;
224
225 void _ParallelMM(double** C, double** A, double** B, int N, int BS, int
       numthreads)
226 {
227   int          rows, extra, start, end, t;
228   pthread_t   *threads;
229   ThreadArgs *args;
230
231   //
232   // Statically divide the N rows into equally-sized chunks, based
233   // on numthreads:
234   //
235   rows  = N / numthreads;
236   extra = N % numthreads;
237   start = 0;   // row dimensions for first thread:
238   end   = rows;
239
240   threads = (pthread_t *) malloc(numthreads * sizeof(pthread_t));
241
242   //
243   // FORK: create threads to multiply rows in parallel...
244   //
245   for (t=0; t < numthreads; t++)
246   {
247     if (t+1 == numthreads)  // last thread does any extra rows:
248       end += extra;
249
250     args = (ThreadArgs *)malloc(sizeof(ThreadArgs));
251     args->A = A;
```

```
252    args->B = B;
253    args->C = C;
254    args->rstart = start;
255    args->rend  = end;
256    args->N    = N;
257    args->BS   = BS;
258
259    pthread_create(&threads[t] , NULL, _DoParallelMM, args);
260
261    start = end;
262    end = start + rows;
263  }
264 //
265  // JOIN: now wait for threads to finish...
266  //
267  for (t=0; t < numthreads; t++)
268  {
269    pthread_join(threads[t] , NULL);
270  }
271
272  free(threads);
273 }
274
275 //
276 // DoMM: code executed by each thread, computing a set of rows of C:
277 //
278 void * _DoParallelMM(void * args)
279 {
280   ThreadArgs * targs;
281   double   ** A, ** B, ** C;
282   int       i, j, k, start, end, N, BS;
283
284   targs = (ThreadArgs * )args;
285
286   A    = targs->A;
287   B    = targs->B;
288   C    = targs->C;
289   start = targs->rstart;
290   end   = targs->rend;
291   N    = targs->N;
292   BS   = targs->BS;
293
294    if (BS < N) // then blocking is needed:
295  {
296
297      int jj, kk, jjEND, kkEND;
298
299      // for each block...
300      for (jj=0; jj<N; jj+=BS)
```

```
301      {
302          jjEND = Min(jj+BS, N);
303
304        // initialize:
305        for (i=start; i<end; i++)
306          for (j=jj; j < jjEND; j++)
307            C[i][j] = 0.0;
308
309        // block multiply:
310        for (kk=0; kk<N; kk+=BS)
311        {
312          kkEND = Min(kk+BS, N);
313
314          for (i=start; i<end; i++)
315            for (k=kk; k < kkEND; k++)
316              for (j=jj; j < jjEND; j++)
317                C[i][j] += (A[i][k] * B[k][j] );
318        }
319       }
320
321    }
322    else // no blocking, just interchange inner-most j and k loops:
323    {
324
325        // initialize:
326        for (i = start; i < end; i++)
327          for (j = 0; j < N; j++)
328            C[i][j] = 0.0;
329
330        // multiply:
331        for (i = start; i < end; i++)
332          for (k = 0; k < N; k++)
333            for (j = 0; j < N; j++)
334              C[i][j] += (A[i][k] * B[k][j] );
335
336    }
337
338    return NULL;
339  }
340  //
341  // CreateAndFillMatrices: fills A and B with predefined values, and
342  // then set TL, TR, BL and BR to the expected top-left, top-right,
343  // bottom-left and bottom-right values after the multiply.
344  //
345  void CreateAndFillMatrices(int N, double*** A, double*** B, double* TL,
346          double* TR, double* BL, double* BR)
347  {
348    double **a;
349    double **b;
350    double   dN;
```

```
350    int       r, c;
351
352    a = New2dMatrix(N, N);
353    b = New2dMatrix(N, N);
354
355    //
356    // A looks like:
357    // 1 1 1 1 ... 1
358    // 2 2 2 2 ... 2
359    // .  .  .  .  ...  .
360    // .  .  .  .  ...  .
361    // N N N N ... N
362    //
363    for (r = 0; r < N /* rows*/; r++)
364      for (c = 0; c < N /* cols*/; c++)
365        a[r][c] = r + 1;
366
367    //
368    // B looks like:
369    // 1 2 3 4 ... N
370    // 1 2 3 4 ... N
371    // .  .  .  .  ...  .
372    // .  .  .  .  ...  .
373    // 1 2 3 4 ... N
374    //
375    for (r = 0; r < N /* rows*/; r++)
376      for (c = 0; c < N /* cols*/; c++)
377        b[r][c] = c + 1;
378
379    //
380    // expected values:
381    //
382    dN = N;  // use double to overflow errors with large N:
383
384    *TL = dN;           // C[0,0]    == Sum(1..1)
385    *TR = dN* dN;       // C[0,N-1]  == Sum(N..N)
386    *BL = dN* dN;       // C[N-1, 0] == Sum(N..N)
387    *BR = dN* dN* dN;   // C[N-1, N-1] == SUM(N^2..N^2)
388
389    // return matrices back to caller:
390    *A = a;
391    *B = b;
392 }
393 //
394 // Checks the results against some expected results:
395 //
396 void CheckResults(int N, double** C, double TL, double TR, double BL,
        double BR)
```

```
397 {
398   int b1, b2, b3, b4;
399
400   b1 = ( fabs(C[0][0]      - TL) < 0.0000001 );
401   b2 = ( fabs(C[0][ N-1]   - TR) < 0.0000001 );
402   b3 = ( fabs(C[N-1][0]    - BL) < 0.0000001 );
403   b4 = ( fabs(C[N-1][N-1]  - BR) < 0.0000001 );
404
405   if (!b1 || !b2 || !b3 || !b4)
406   {
407     printf("** ERROR: matrix multiply yielded incorrect results\n\n");
408     exit(0);
409   }
410 }
411
412
413 //
414 // processCmdLineArgs:
415 //
416 void ProcessCmdLineArgs(int argc, char* argv[])
417 {
418   int i;
419
420   for (i = 1; i < argc; i++)
421   {
422
423     if (strcmp(argv[i], "-?") == 0) // help:
424     {
425       printf("**Usage: mm-cache[-?] [-n MatrixSize] [-b BlockSize]
426         [-t NumThreads]\n\n");
426       exit(0);
427     }
428     else if ((strcmp(argv[i], "-n") == 0) && (i+1 < argc)) // matrix size:
429     {
430       i++;
431       _matrixSize = atoi(argv[i]);
432       _setMatrixSize = 1; // true:
433     }
434     else if ((strcmp(argv[i], "-b") == 0) && (i+1 < argc)) // block size:
435     {
436       i++;
437       _blockSize = atoi(argv[i]);
438       _setBlockSize = 1; // true:
439     }
440     else if ((strcmp(argv[i], "-t") == 0) && (i+1 < argc)) // matrix size:
441     {
442       i++;
443       _numThreads = atoi(argv[i]);
444     }
```

```
445        else // error: unknown arg
446      {
447        printf("**Unknown argument: '%s'\n", argv[i] );
448        printf("**Usage: mm-cache[-?] [-n MatrixSize] [-b BlockSize]
             [-t NumThreads]\n\n");
449        exit(0);
450      }
451
452    } //for
453 }
454
455
456 //
457 // Matrix allocation functions:
458 //
459
460 //
461 // New2dMatrix: allocates a 2D matrix of size ROWSxCOLS, which is really
462 // a 1D array of row pointers into a large, contiguous block of 1D memory.
463 // For example, in ASCII art, here's a 3x5 array:
464 //
465 //           -------------------------------
466 //           | | | | | | | | | | | | | | | |
467 //           -------------------------------
468 //            ^           ^           ^
469 //            |           |           |
470 // ---        |           |           |
471 // |----------           |           |
472 // ---                   |           |
473 // |---------------------           |
474 // ---                              |
475 // |--------------------------------
476 // ---
477 //
478 // Much more efficient for caching, if using MPI to send messages, etc.
479 //
480 double **New2dMatrix(int ROWS, int COLS)
481 {
482   double **matrix;
483   double  *elements;
484   int       r;
485
486   //
487   // for efficiency of both allocation and transmission, we allocate the
488   // matrix as 1 large chunk of memory, then set the row pointers into
489   // this chunk:
490   //
491   matrix = (double **) malloc(ROWS * sizeof(double*));
```

```
492   elements = (double *) malloc(ROWS * COLS * sizeof(double));
493
494 for (r = 0; r < ROWS; r++)
495    matrix[r] = &elements[r * COLS];
496
497   return matrix;
498 }
499
500
501 //
502 // Delete2dMatrix: frees memory associated with 2D matrix allocated by
503 // New2dMatrix.
504 //
505 void Delete2dMatrix(double **matrix)
506 {
507   free(matrix[0]);
508   free(matrix);
509 }
510
511
512 //
513 // my_clock: clock function for Windows and Linux, returning time in secs
514 //
515 double my_clock()
516 {
517 #ifdef WINDOWS
518   return ((double) clock()) / CLOCKS_PER_SEC;
519 #endif
520
521 #ifdef LINUX
522   struct timeval t;
523
524   gettimeofday(&t, NULL);
525
526   return (1.0e-6 * t.tv_usec) + t.tv_sec;
527 #endif
528 }
```

PRIMES CODE WITH RACE CONDITIONS

```
1 /* primes.c */
2
3 //
4 // Determines prime numbers, naively...
5 //
6 // Usage:
7 //   primes [-?] [-t NumThreads]
8 //
9
```

```
10  #define LINUX
11  /// #define WINDOWS
12
13  #include <stdio.h>
14  #include <stdlib.h>
15  #include <string.h>
16  #include <math.h>
17  #include <time.h>
18
19  #ifdef LINUX
20  #include <sys/time.h>
21  #endif
22
23  #include "pthread.h"
24
25
26  //
27  // Function prototypes:
28  //
29  void PrimeNumberSearch(long start, long end);
30  int  isPrime(long n);
31
32  void CreateList();
33  void AddToList(long l);
34  void SortList();
35  void DumpList();
36  void FreeList();
37
38  void   ProcessCmdLineArgs(int argc, char* argv[]);
39  double my_clock();
40
41
42  //
43  // Globals:
44  //
45  int _numThreads;
46
47  //
48  // main:
49  //
50  int main(int argc, char *argv[])
51  {
52    double startTime, stopTime, time;
53    long    start, end;
54
55    //
56    // Set defaults, process environment & cmd-line args:
57    //
```

```
58   _numThreads = 1;    // pthread_num_processors_np();
59
60   // number range to search:
61   start = 2;
62   end   = 2500000;  // 2.5MB:
63
64   ProcessCmdLineArgs(argc, argv);
65
66   printf("** Search Application for Prime Numbers **\n\n");
67   printf("   Search space: %ld .. %ld\n", start, end);
68   printf("   Num threads: %d\n", _numThreads);
69   printf("\n");
70   printf("** Searching...\n\n");
71
72   //
73   // Create a list for holding prime numbers we find:
74   //
75   CreateList();
76
77   //
78   // Start clock and search:
79   //
80   startTime = my_clock();
81
82   PrimeNumberSearch(start, end);
83
84   stopTime = my_clock();
85   time = stopTime - startTime;
86
87   //
88   // Done, check results and output timing:
89   //
90   printf("** Done!  Time: %4.2f secs\n", time);
91   DumpList();
92
93   //
94   // cleanup:
95   //
96   FreeList();
97
98   pthread_exit(NULL); // aka return:
99 }
100 //
101 // PrimeNumberSearch:
102 //
103 void PrimeNumberSearch(long start, long end)
104 {
105   long p;
106
```

```
107    for (p = start; p <= end; p++)
108    {
109      if (isPrime(p))
110        AddToList(p);
111    }
112  }
113
114
115  //
116  // isPrime: returns true if n is prime, false if not
117  //
118  int isPrime(long n)
119  {
120    long start, end, i;
121
122    start = 2;
123    end = (long) floor((sqrt((double) n) + 1));
124
125    // see if any numbers divide evenly; if so, not a prime:
126    for (i = start; i < end; i++)
127      if (n % i == 0)
128        return 0; // it's not prime, return now:
129
130    return 1; // it's prime!
131  }
132
133
134  //
135  // List functions: create, add, sort, dump, and free
136  //
137  long * _LIST;
138  long  _LISTSIZE;
139  long  _LISTCOUNT;
140
141  void CreateList()
142  {
143    // we create a list of size 1000 initially, and then double as needed:
144    _LISTSIZE = 1000;
145    _LIST = (long *) malloc(_LISTSIZE * sizeof(long));
146
147    _LISTCOUNT = 0;
148  }
149
150  void AddToList(long l)
151  {
152    // is list full? if so, double in size and copy stuff over:
153    if (_LISTCOUNT == _LISTSIZE) // full
154    {
155      long * temp = (long *) malloc(2 * _LISTSIZE * sizeof(long));
```

```
156    long i;
157
158    for (i = 0; i < _LISTSIZE; i++)
159      temp[i] = _LIST[i];
160
161    free(_LIST);
162
163    _LIST = temp;
164    _LISTSIZE = 2 * _LISTSIZE;
165  }
166
167  // now add to end:
168  _LIST[_LISTCOUNT] = 1;
169  _LISTCOUNT++;
170 }
171
172 // compare function for qsort below:
173 int _compare(const void * a1, const void * a2)
174 {
175   long l1, l2;
176   l1 = * ((long *) a1);
177   l2 = * ((long *) a2);
178
179   // for ascending order, return positive if l1 > l2:
180   if (l1 > l2)
181     return 1;
182   else if (l1 == l2)
183     return 0;
184   else
185     return -1;
186 }
187
188 void SortList()
189 {
190   qsort(_LIST, _LISTCOUNT, sizeof(long), _compare);
191 }
192
193 void DumpList()
194 {
195   //
196   // dumps first and last 4 primes in the list...
197   //
198   printf("** Primes found: %ld\n", _LISTCOUNT);
199   printf("   %ld\n", _LIST[0] );
200   printf("   %ld\n", _LIST[1] );
201   printf("   %ld\n", _LIST[2] );
202   printf("   %ld\n", _LIST[3] );
203   printf("   .\n");
204   printf("   .\n");
```

```
205    printf("    .\n");
206    printf("    %ld\n", _LIST[ _LISTCOUNT-4 ] );
207    printf("    %ld\n", _LIST[ _LISTCOUNT-3 ] );
208    printf("    %ld\n", _LIST[ _LISTCOUNT-2 ] );
209    printf("    %ld\n", _LIST[ _LISTCOUNT-1 ] );
210    printf("\n\n\n");
211  }
212
213  void FreeList()
214  {
215    free( _LIST );
216
217    _LIST = NULL;
218    _LISTSIZE = 0;
219    _LISTCOUNT = 0;
220  }
221
222
223  //
224  // processCmdLineArgs:
225  //
226  void ProcessCmdLineArgs(int argc, char* argv[])
227  {
228    int i;
229
230    for (i = 1; i < argc; i++)
231    {
232
233      if (strcmp(argv[i], "-?") == 0)  // help:
234      {
235        printf("**Usage: primes [-?] [ -t NumThreads] \n\n");
236        exit(0);
237      }
238      else if ((strcmp(argv[i], "-t") == 0) && (i+1 < argc))  // matrix size:
239      {
240        i++;
241        _numThreads = atoi(argv[i] );
242      }
243      else  // error: unknown arg
244      {
245        printf("**Unknown argument: '%s'\n", argv[i] );
246        printf("**Usage: primes [-?] [-t NumThreads] \n\n");
247        exit(0);
248      }
249
250    } //for
251  }
252
253
```

```
254  //
255  // my_clock: clock function for Windows and Linux, returning time in secs
256  //
257  double my_clock()
258  {
259  #ifdef WINDOWS
260    return ((double) clock()) / CLOCKS_PER_SEC;
261  #endif
262
263  #ifdef LINUX
264    struct timeval t;
265
266    gettimeofday(&t, NULL);
267
268    return (1.0e-6 * t.tv_usec) + t.tv_sec;
269  #endif
270  }
```

PRIMES CODE WITH RACE CONDITIONS FIXED

```
 1  /* primes.c */
 2
 3  //
 4  // Determines prime numbers, naively... This is a parallel version,
 5  // creating one thread per core to search for primes in parallel.
 6  //
 7  // Usage:
 8  //   primes [-?] [-t NumThreads]
 9  //
10
11  #define LINUX
12  // #define WINDOWS
13
14  #include <stdio.h>
15  #include <stdlib.h>
16  #include <string.h>
17  #include <math.h>
18  #include <time.h>
19
20  #ifdef LINUX
21  #include <sys/time.h>
22  #endif
23
24  #include "pthread.h"
25
26  //
27  // Function prototypes:
28  //
29  void  PrimeNumberSearch(long start, long end, int numthreads);
```

```
30  void * _DoPrimeNumberSearch (void * args) ;
31  int   isPrime (long n) ;
32
33  void CreateList () ;
34  void AddToList (long l) ;
35  void SortList () ;
36  void DumpList () ;
37  void FreeList () ;
38
39  void  ProcessCmdLineArgs (int argc, char* argv[ ] ) ;
40  double my_clock () ;
41
42
43  //
44  // Globals:
45  //
46  int _numThreads;
47
48  //
49  // main:
50  //
51  int main (int argc, char * argv[ ] )
52  {
53    double startTime, stopTime, time;
54    long  start, end;
55
56    //
57    // Set defaults, process environment & cmd-line args:
58    //
59    // _numThreads = 1;
60    // _numThreads = pthread_num_processors_np () ;  // 1 per core:
61    _numThreads = 4;
62
63    // number range to search:
64    start = 2;
65    end  = 2500000;  // 2.5MB:
66
67    ProcessCmdLineArgs (argc, argv) ;
68
69    printf ("** Search Application for Prime Numbers **\n\n") ;
70    printf ("  Search space: %ld .. %ld\n", start, end) ;
71    printf ("  Num threads: %d\n", _numThreads) ;
72    printf ("\n") ;
73    printf ("** Searching...\n\n") ;
74
75    //
76    // Create a list for holding prime numbers we find:
77    //
```

```
 78   CreateList();
 79
 80   //
 81   // Start clock and search:
 82   //
 83   startTime = my_clock();
 84
 85   PrimeNumberSearch(start, end, _numThreads);
 86
 87   //
 88   // Note: since we did in parallel, need to sort the list:
 89   //
 90   SortList();
 91
 92   stopTime = my_clock();
 93   time = stopTime - startTime;
 94
 95   //
 96   // Done, check results and output timing:
 97   //
 98   printf("** Done!  Time: %4.2f secs\n", time);
 99   DumpList();
100 //
101   // cleanup:
102   //
103   FreeList();
104
105   pthread_exit(NULL); // aka return:
106 }
107
108
109 //
110 // PrimeNumberSearch:
111 //
112 typedef struct ThreadArgs
113 {
114   long              end;              // end of search space:
115   long             *candidate;        // next candidate to check:
116   pthread_mutex_t *candidate_lock; // lock to protect candidate:
117   pthread_mutex_t *list_lock;   // lock to protect list:
118 } ThreadArgs;
119
120 void PrimeNumberSearch(long start, long end, int numthreads)$$$$$
121 {
122   int              t;
123   long             candidate;
124   ThreadArgs      *args;
125   pthread_t       *threads;
126   pthread_mutex_t list_lock, candidate_lock;
127
```

```
128    // for keeping track of each thread:
129    threads = (pthread_t *) malloc(numthreads * sizeof(pthread_t));
130
131    // create locks for threads to use:
132    pthread_mutex_init(&list_lock, NULL);
133    pthread_mutex_init(&candidate_lock, NULL);
134
135    //
136    // FORK: create threads to search in parallel...
137    //
138    candidate = start;
139
140    for (t=0; t < numthreads; t++)
141    {
142      args = (ThreadArgs *)malloc(sizeof(ThreadArgs));
143      args->end = end;
144      args->candidate = &candidate;
145      args->candidate_lock = &candidate_lock;
146      args->list_lock      = &list_lock;
147
148      pthread_create(&threads[t] , NULL, _DoPrimeNumberSearch, args);
149    }
150    //
151    // JOIN: now wait for threads to finish...
152    //
153    for (t=0; t < numthreads; t++)
154    {
155      pthread_join(threads[t] , NULL);
156    }
157
158    free(threads);
159  }
160
161  void * _DoPrimeNumberSearch(void * args)
162  {
163    ThreadArgs * targs;
164    long         p;
165
166    targs = (ThreadArgs * )args;
167
168    //
169    // Grab a candidate, test for primeness, repeat:
170    //
171    while (1 /*true*/)
172    {
173      //
174      // grab a candidate: since this is a shared variable, we need to
175      // protect resulting critical section with a lock:
176      //
177      pthread_mutex_lock(targs->candidate_lock);
```

```
178        p = *targs->candidate;      // grab next candidate:
179        *targs->candidate = p+1;   // advance for next thread:
180      pthread_mutex_unlock(targs->candidate_lock);
181
182      if (p > targs->end)  // outside of search range, time to stop:
183        break;
184
185      if (isPrime(p))
186      {
187        //
188        // we have found a prime number, but list is another shared
189        // resource, so we need to lock across access to data
190        // structure:
191        //
192        pthread_mutex_lock(targs->list_lock);
193          AddToList(p);
194        pthread_mutex_unlock(targs->list_lock);
195      }
196    }
197
198    // cleanup:
199    free(targs);
200
201    return NULL;
202 }
203
204
205 //
206 // isPrime: returns true if n is prime, false if not
207 //
208 int isPrime(long n)
209 {
210    long start, end, i;
211
212    start = 2;
213    end = (long) floor((sqrt((double) n) + 1));
214
215    // see if any numbers divide evenly; if so, not a prime:
216    for (i = start; i < end; i++)
217      if (n % i == 0)
218        return 0; // it's not prime, return now:
219
220    return 1; // it's prime!
221 }
222
223
224 //
225 // List functions: create, add, sort, dump, and free
226 //
227 long *_LIST;
```

```
228  long  _LISTSIZE;
229  long  _LISTCOUNT;
230
231  void CreateList ()
232  {
233    // we create a list of size 1000 initially, and then double as needed:
234    _LISTSIZE = 1000;
235    _LIST = (long *) malloc (_LISTSIZE * sizeof (long));
236
237    _LISTCOUNT = 0;
238  }
239
240  void AddToList (long l)
241  {
242    // is list full? if so, double in size and copy stuff over:
243    if (_LISTCOUNT == _LISTSIZE)  // full
244    {
245      long * temp = (long *) malloc (2 * _LISTSIZE * sizeof (long));
246      long i;
247
248      for (i = 0; i < _LISTSIZE; i++)
249        temp[i] = _LIST[i] ;
250
251      free (_LIST);
252
253      _LIST = temp;
254      _LISTSIZE = 2 * _LISTSIZE;
255    }
256    // now add to end:
257    _LIST[ _LISTCOUNT ] = l;
258    _LISTCOUNT++;
259  }
260
261  // compare function for qsort below:
262  int _compare (const void * a1, const void * a2)
263  {
264    long l1, l2;
265    l1 = * ((long *) a1);
266    l2 = * ((long *) a2);
267
268    // for ascending order, return positive if l1 > l2:
269    if (l1 > l2)
270      return 1;
271    else if (l1 == l2)
272      return 0;
273    else
274      return -1;
275  }
276
```

```
277  void SortList()
278  {
279    qsort(_LIST, _LISTCOUNT, sizeof(long), _compare);
280  }
281
282  void DumpList()
283  {
284    //
285    // dumps first and last 4 primes in the list...
286    //
287    printf("** Primes found: %ld\n", _LISTCOUNT);
288    printf("  %ld\n", _LIST[0] );
289    printf("  %ld\n", _LIST[1] );
290    printf("  %ld\n", _LIST[2] );
291    printf("  %ld\n", _LIST[3] );
292    printf("  .\n");
293    printf("  .\n");
294    printf("  .\n");
295    printf("  %ld\n", _LIST[ _LISTCOUNT-4 ] );
296    printf("  %ld\n", _LIST[ _LISTCOUNT-3 ] );
297    printf("  %ld\n", _LIST[ _LISTCOUNT-2 ] );
298    printf("  %ld\n", _LIST[ _LISTCOUNT-1 ] );
299    printf("\n\n\n");
300  }
301  void FreeList()
302  {
303    free( _LIST );
304
305    _LIST = NULL;
306    _LISTSIZE = 0;
307    _LISTCOUNT = 0;
308  }
309
310
311  //
312  // processCmdLineArgs:
313  //
314  void ProcessCmdLineArgs(int argc, char* argv[] )
315  {
316    int i;
317
318    for (i = 1; i < argc; i++)
319    {
320
321      if (strcmp(argv[i] , "-?") == 0)  // help:
322      {
323        printf("** Usage: primes [-?] [-t NumThreads] \n\n");
324        exit(0);
325      }
```

```
326      else if ((strcmp(argv[i], "-t") == 0) && (i+1 < argc)) // matrix size:
327      {
328        i++;
329        _numThreads = atoi(argv[i]);
330      }
331      else // error: unknown arg
332      {
333        printf("**Unknown argument: '%s'\n", argv[i]);
334        printf("**Usage: primes [-?] [-t NumThreads]\n\n");
335        exit(0);
336      }
337    } //for
338 }
339
340 //
341 // my_clock: clock function for Windows and Linux, returning time in secs
342 //
343 double my_clock()
344 {
345 #ifdef WINDOWS
346    return ((double) clock()) / CLOCKS_PER_SEC;
347 #endif
348
349 #ifdef LINUX
350    struct timeval t;
351
352    gettimeofday(&t, NULL);
353
354    return (1.0e-6 * t.tv_usec) + t.tv_sec;
355 #endif
356 }
```

CONWAY'S GAME OF LIFE UNOPTIMIZED

```
 1 #include <pthread.h>
 2 #include <stdlib.h>
 3 #include <time.h>
 4 #include <stdbool.h>
 5 #include <stdio.h>
 6 #include <unistd.h>
 7 #include "string.h"
 8 #include "simple_barrier.h"
 9
10 #define LINUX
11
12 #ifdef LINUX
13 #include <sys/time.h>
14 #endif
15
```

```
16  void parse_arguments(int argc, char* argv[ ]);
17
18  void sequential_game_of_life(bool ** ib, bool ** cb);
19  void parallel_game_of_life(bool ** ib, bool ** cb);
20
21  // Board computation functions
22  void compute_whole_board(bool ** initial_board, bool **
        computed_board, int width, int height);
23  void* compute_cells(void * args);
24  static inline void compute_cell(int cell_row, int cell_column, bool **
        ib, bool ** cb);
25
26  // Board helper functions.
27  bool ** create_board(int width, int height);
28  void seed_random_board(bool **, int, int);
29  void seed_test_board(bool **, int, int);
30  void print_board(bool ** board, int width, int height);
31  bool compare_boards(bool ** b1, bool ** b2, int width, int height);
32  double get_time();
33
34  //Globals
35  int g_rows;
36  int g_columns;
37  int g_threads;
38  int g_iterations;
39  bool g_display;
40  bool g_randomize_board;
41  bool g_test;
42
43  struct thread_args{
44        bool ** ib;
45        bool ** cb;
46        pthread_mutex_t * next_cell_lock;
47        int * next_cell;
48  } thread_args;
49  void parse_arguments(int argc, char* argv[ ]) {
50        int i;
51        for (i = 1; i < argc; i++) {
52              if (strcmp(argv[i], "-?") == 0) { //Help
53                    printf("Usage: [-?] [-n BoardSize] [-t
                          ThreadNumber] [-t Iterations] [-d] [-z] \n");
54                    exit(0);
55              } else if (strcmp(argv[i], "-n") == 0) { // Board size.
                    For now we will only support square boards.
56                    i++;
57                    g_rows = atoi(argv[i]);
58                    g_columns = g_rows;
59              } else if (strcmp(argv[i], "-t") == 0) { // Thread count
60                    i++;
61                    g_threads = atoi(argv[i]);
```

```
62                  } else if (strcmp(argv[i], "-i") == 0) { // Iterations
63                      i++;
64                      g_iterations = atoi(argv[i]);
65                  } else if (strcmp(argv[i], "-d") == 0) { // Display
66                      g_display = true;
67                  } else if (strcmp(argv[i], "-r") == 0) { // Randomize
                          board
68                      g_randomize_board = true;
69                  } else if (strcmp(argv[i], "-z") == 0) { // Test against
              sequential algorithm
70                      g_test = true;
71                  } else {
72                      printf("Unknown argument: '%s'\n", argv[i]);
73                      printf("Usage: [-?] [-n BoardSize]
                          [-t ThreadNumber] [ -t Iterations] [-d] [-z] \n");
74                      exit(0);
75                  }
76          }
77
78      printf("Arguments:\n\tBoard Size: %d by %d\n\tThread Count: %d
    \n\tIterations %d\n\tDisplay: %d\n\tRandomize Board: %d\tTesting
    against sequential: %d\n\n", g_rows, g_columns, g_threads,
    g_iterations, g_display, g_randomize_board, g_test);
79  }
80  int main(int argc, char* argv[]) {
81
82      double start_time, end_time, time;
83      g_rows = 20;
84      g_columns= 20;
85      g_threads = 1;
86      g_iterations = 100;
87      g_display = false;
88      g_randomize_board = false;
89      g_test = false;
90
91      parse_arguments(argc, argv);
92
93      //Clean the input
94      if (g_threads < 1) g_threads = 1;
95      if (g_threads > 128) g_threads = 128;
96      if (g_rows < 2) g_rows = 2;
97      if (g_columns < 2) g_columns = 2;
98      if (!g_randomize_board) {
99          if (g_columns < 9 || g_rows < 9) {
100             printf("Rows and/or Column count must be greater
    than 9 to populate test board. Setting n = 10\n");
101             g_rows = 10;
102             g_columns = 10;
103         }
104     }
```

```
105
106          //For simplicity, each board gets boundary edges.
107          bool ** initial_board1 = create_board(g_columns+2, g_rows+2);
108          bool ** computed_board1 = create_board(g_columns+2, g_rows+2);
109          bool ** initial_board2;
110          bool ** computed_board2;
111
112
113          if (g_randomize_board) {
114                  seed_random_board(initial_board1, g_columns, g_rows);
115          } else {
116                  seed_test_board(initial_board1, g_columns, g_rows);
117          }
118          if (g_test) {
119                  initial_board2 = create_board(g_columns+2, g_rows+2);
120                  computed_board2 = create_board(g_columns+2, g_rows+2);
121                  if (g_randomize_board) {
122                          seed_random_board(initial_board2, g_columns,
                                 g_rows);
123                  } else {
124                          seed_test_board(initial_board2, g_columns,
                                 g_rows);
125                  }
126          }
127
128          start_time = get_time();
129          parallel_game_of_life(initial_board1, computed_board1);
130          end_time = get_time();
131          time = end_time - start_time;
132
133
134          printf("\n Simulation Complete! Execution time: %4.2f secs\n
             \n", time);
135
136          if (g_test) {
137                  printf("\nRunning sequential Game of Life for
                         comparison...\n");
138
139                  sequential_game_of_life(initial_board2,
                         computed_board2);
140
141                  if (compare_boards(initial_board1, initial_board2,
                         g_columns, g_rows)) {
142                          printf("Result of parallel and sequential
                                 algorithm are equal. Test passed!\n");
143                  } else {
144                          printf("Results of parallel and sequential
                                 algorithm are NOT equal. Test failed!\n
                                 \nSequential:\n");
145                          print_board(initial_board2, g_columns, g_rows);
```

```
146                        printf("Parallel:\n");
147                        print_board(initial_board1, g_columns,
     g_rows);
148                }
149        }
150        return 0;
151 }
152
153 void sequential_game_of_life(bool ** ib, bool ** cb) {
154
155        for (int i = 0; i < g_iterations; i++) {
156
157                compute_whole_board(ib, cb, g_columns, g_rows);
158
159                bool ** tmp = cb;
160                cb = ib;
161                ib = tmp;
162        }
163 }
164 void parallel_game_of_life(bool ** ib, bool ** cb) {
165
166        pthread_t * threads;
167        pthread_mutex_t * next_cell_lock;
168        int * next_cell;
169
170        next_cell_lock = (pthread_mutex_t *) malloc(sizeof
     (pthread_mutex_t));
171        next_cell = (int *) malloc(sizeof(int));
172
173        * next_cell = 0;
174
175        for (int itr = 0; itr < g_iterations; itr++) {
176                threads = (pthread_t *) malloc(g_threads * sizeof
     (pthread_t));
177                // Compose thread arguments and dispatch the threads.
178                for (int i = 0; i < g_threads; i++) {
179                        struct thread_args * args;
180                        args = (struct thread_args*) malloc
                                (sizeof(struct thread_args));
181                        args->ib = ib;
182                        args->cb = cb;
183                        args->next_cell_lock = next_cell_lock;
184                        args->next_cell = next_cell;
185
186                        pthread_create(&threads[i] , NULL, compute_cells,
     args);
187                }
188                for (int i = 0; i < g_threads; i++) {
189                        pthread_join(threads[i] , NULL);
190                }
```

```
191                    //Free our now joined threads.
192                    free(threads);
193
194                    //Swap boards.
195                    bool ** tmp = cb;
196                    cb = ib;
197                    ib = tmp;
198
199                    //Reset cell count;
200                    *next_cell = 0;
201                    if (g_display) {
202                            print_board(ib, g_rows, g_columns);
203                            sleep(1);
204                    }
205            }
206 }
207
208 void* compute_cells(void * args) {
209        struct thread_args * thread_args = (struct thread_args*) args;
210        bool ** ib = thread_args->ib;
211        bool ** cb = thread_args->cb;
212        pthread_mutex_t * next_cell_lock =
           thread_args->next_cell_lock;
213        int *next_cell = thread_args->next_cell;
214
215        int total_cells;
216        int next_cell_row;
217        int next_cell_column;
218        total_cells = g_rows * g_columns;
219        int current_cell = 0;
220
221        do {
222                //Determine the next cell to compute.
223                pthread_mutex_lock(next_cell_lock);
224                if (total_cells - *next_cell > 0) {
225                        current_cell = (*next_cell)++;
226                } else {
227                        current_cell = -1;
228                }
229                pthread_mutex_unlock(next_cell_lock);
230
231                if (current_cell != -1) {
232                        next_cell_row = current_cell / g_columns;
233                        next_cell_column = current_cell % g_columns;
234
235                        //Compute the cell value and update our table.
   Add 1 to each to account for our boarder
236                        compute_cell(next_cell_row + 1,
   next_cell_column + 1, ib, cb);
237                }
```

```
238            //Keep looping until we go past the last cell.
239        } while (current_cell > - 1);
240  }
241  void compute_cell(int r, int c, bool ** ib, bool ** cb) {
242        int value = 0;
243        if (ib[r-1][c-1] ) { value++; }
244        if (ib[r][c-1] ) { value++; }
245        if (ib[r+1][c-1] ) { value++; }
246
247        if (ib[r-1][c] ) { value++; }
248        if (ib[r+1][c] ) { value++; }
249
250        if (ib[r-1][c+1] ) { value++; }
251        if (ib[r][c+1] ) { value++; }
252        if (ib[r+1][c+1] ) { value++; }
253
254        if (ib[r][c] ) {
255                if (value < 2) { cb[r][c] = false; }
256                if (value == 2 || value == 3) { cb[r][c] = true; }
257                if (value > 3) { cb[r][c] = false; }
258        } else {
259                if (value == 3) {
260                        cb[r][c] = true;
261                } else {
262                        cb[r][c] = false;
263                }
264        }
265        return;
266  }
267  void compute_whole_board(bool ** initial_board, bool **
     computed_board, int width, int height) {
268        for (int i = 1; i <= height; i++) {
269                for (int j = 1; j <= width; j++) {
270
271                        int value = 0;
272
273                        if (initial_board[i-1][j-1] ) { value++; }
274                        if (initial_board[i][j-1] ) { value++; }
275                        if (initial_board[i+1][j-1] ) { value++; }
276
277                        if (initial_board[i-1][j] ) { value++; }
278                        if (initial_board[i+1][j] ) { value++; }
279
280                        if (initial_board[i-1][j+1] ) { value++; }
281                        if (initial_board[i][j+1] ) { value++; }
282                        if (initial_board[i+1][j+1] ) { value++; }
283
284
285                        if (initial_board[i][j] ) {
```

```
286                              if (value < 2) { computed_board[i][j] =
                                 false; }
287                              if (value == 2 || value == 3) {
                                 computed_board[i][j] = true; }
288                              if (value > 3) { computed_board[i][j] =
                                 false; }
289                      } else {
290                              if (value == 3) {
291                                      computed_board[i][j] = true;
292                              } else {
293                                      computed_board[i][j] = false;
294                              }
295                      }
296              }
297      }
298 }
```

CONWAY'S GAME OF LIFE OPTIMIZED

```
 1 #include <pthread.h>
 2 #include <stdlib.h>
 3 #include <time.h>
 4 #include <stdbool.h>
 5 #include <stdio.h>
 6 #include <unistd.h>
 7 #include "string.h"
 8 #include "simple_barrier.h"
 9
10 #define LINUX
11
12 #ifdef LINUX
13 #include <sys/time.h>
14 #endif
15
16
17 void parse_arguments(int argc, char* argv[]);
18
19 void sequential_game_of_life(bool ** ib, bool ** cb);
20 void parallel_game_of_life(bool ** ib, bool ** cb);
21
22 // Board computation functions
23 void compute_whole_board(bool ** initial_board, bool **
   computed_board, int width, int height);
24 void* compute_cells(void * args);
25 static inline void compute_cell(int cell_row, int cell_column, bool **
   ib, bool ** cb);
26
27 // Board helper functions.
```

```
28  bool ** create_board(int width, int height);
29  void seed_random_board(bool **, int, int);
30  void seed_test_board(bool **, int, int);
31  void print_board(bool **board, int width, int height);
32  bool compare_boards(bool **b1, bool **b2, int width, int height);
33
34  double get_time();
35
36  //Globals
37  int g_rows;
38  int g_columns;
39  int g_threads;
40  int g_iterations;
41  bool g_display;
42  bool g_randomize_board;
43  bool g_test;
44
45  struct thread_args{
46        bool ** ib;
47        bool ** cb;
48        int start_row;
49        int end_row;
50        struct simple_barrier * barrier;
51  } thread_args;
52  void parse_arguments(int argc, char* argv[ ]) {
53        int i;
54        for (i = 1; i < argc; i++) {
55              if (strcmp(argv[i] , "-?") == 0) { //Help
56                    printf("Usage:[-?] [ -n BoardSize] [-t
                      ThreadNumber] [-t Iterations] [-d] [-z] \n");
57                    exit(0);
58              } else if (strcmp(argv[i] , "-n") == 0) { // Board size.
                  For now we will only support square boards.
59                    i++;
60                    g_rows = atoi(argv[i] );
61                    g_columns = g_rows;
62              } else if (strcmp(argv[i] , "-t") == 0) { // Thread count
63                    i++;
64                    g_threads = atoi(argv[i] );
65              } else if (strcmp(argv[i] , "-i") == 0) { // Iterations
66                    i++;
67                    g_iterations = atoi(argv[i] );
68              } else if (strcmp(argv[i] , "-d") == 0) { // Display
69                    g_display = true;
70              } else if (strcmp(argv[i] , "-r") == 0) { // Randomize
                  board
71                    g_randomize_board = true;
```

```
72                   } else if (strcmp(argv[i] , "-z") == 0) { // Test against
                     sequential algorithm
73                          g_test = true;
74                   } else {
75                          printf("Unknown argument: '%s'\n", argv[i] );
76                          printf("Usage: [-?] [ -n BoardSize] [-t
                            ThreadNumber] [-t Iterations] [-d] [-z] \n");
77                          exit(0);
78                   }
79            }
80        printf("Arguments:\n\tBoard Size: %d by %d\n\tThread Count: %d
      \n\tIterations %d\n\tDisplay: %d\n\tRandomize Board: %d\tTesting
      against sequential: %d\n\n", g_rows, g_columns, g_threads,
      g_iterations, g_display, g_randomize_board, g_test);
81  }
82  int main(int argc, char* argv[] ) {
83
84        double start_time, end_time, time;
85        g_rows = 20;
86        g_columns = 20;
87        g_threads = 1;
88        g_iterations = 100;
89        g_display = false;
90        g_randomize_board = false;
91        g_test = false;
92
93        parse_arguments(argc, argv);
94
95        //Clean the input
96        if (g_threads < 1) g_threads = 1;
97        if (g_threads > 128) g_threads = 128;
98        if (g_rows < 2) g_rows = 2;
99        if (g_columns < 2) g_columns = 2;
100       if (!g_randomize_board) {
101              if (g_columns < 9 || g_rows < 9) {
102                     printf("Rows and/or Column count must be greater
                         than 9 to populate test board. Setting n = 10\n");
103                     g_rows = 10;
104                     g_columns = 10;
105              }
106       }
107
108
109       //For simplicity, each board gets boundary edges.
110       bool ** initial_board1 = create_board(g_columns+2, g_rows+2);
111       bool ** computed_board1 = create_board(g_columns+2, g_rows+2);
112       bool ** initial_board2;
113       bool ** computed_board2;
114
115
```

```
116            if (g_randomize_board) {
117                    seed_random_board(initial_board1, g_columns, g_rows);
118            } else {
119                    seed_test_board(initial_board1, g_columns, g_rows);
120            }
121            if (g_test) {
122                    initial_board2 = create_board(g_columns+2, g_rows+2);
123                    computed_board2 = create_board(g_columns+2, g_rows+2);
124                    if (g_randomize_board) {
125                            seed_random_board(initial_board2, g_columns,
                               g_rows);
126                    } else {
127                            seed_test_board(initial_board2, g_columns,
                               g_rows);
128                    }
129            }
130
131
132            start_time = get_time();
133            parallel_game_of_life(initial_board1, computed_board1);
134            end_time = get_time();
135            time = end_time - start_time;
136
137            printf("\n Simulation Complete! Execution time: %4.2f secs\n
               \n", time);
138
139            if (g_test) {
140                    printf("\nRunning sequential Game of Life for
                       comparison...\n");
141
142                    sequential_game_of_life(initial_board2,
                       computed_board2);
143
144                    if (compare_boards(initial_board1, initial_board2,
                       g_columns, g_rows)) {
145                            printf("Result of parallel and sequential
                               algorithm are equal. Test passed!\n");
146                    } else {
147                            printf("Results of parallel and sequential
       algorithm are NOT equal. Test failed!\n\nSequential:\n");
148                            print_board(initial_board2, g_columns, g_rows);
149                            printf("Parallel:\n");
150                            print_board(initial_board1, g_columns, g_rows);
151                    }
152            }
153            return 0;
154    }
155    void sequential_game_of_life(bool ** ib, bool ** cb) {
156
157            for (int i = 0; i < g_iterations; i++) {
```

```
158
159                    compute_whole_board(ib, cb, g_columns, g_rows);
160
161                    bool ** tmp = cb;
162                    cb = ib;
163                    ib = tmp;
164            }
165 }
166
167 void parallel_game_of_life(bool ** ib, bool ** cb) {
168
169            pthread_t * threads;
170            struct simple_barrier * barrier;
171            int rows_per_thread = g_rows / g_threads;
172            int rows_per_thread_remainder = g_rows % g_threads;
173
174            threads = (pthread_t *) malloc(g_threads * sizeof(pthread_t));
175            barrier = (struct simple_barrier*) malloc(sizeof(struct
               simple_barrier));
176
177            simple_barrier_init(barrier, g_threads);
178
179            for (int i = 0; i < g_threads; i++) {
180                    struct thread_args * args;
181                    args = (struct thread_args*) malloc(sizeof
       (struct thread_args));
182                    args->ib = ib;
183                    args->cb = cb;
184                    //Add one to account for our grids uncomputed edges.
185                    args->start_row = (i * rows_per_thread) + 1;
186                    //The last thread gets any remainder rows.
187                    if (i + 1 == g_threads) {
188
189                            args->end_row = args->start_row +
                                rows_per_thread - 1 + rows_per_thread_remainder;
190                    } else {
191                            args->end_row = args->start_row+rows_per_thread-1;
192                    }
193                    args->barrier = barrier;
194
195
196                    pthread_create(&threads[i] , NULL, compute_cells, args);
197            }
198
199
200            for (int i = 0; i < g_threads; i++) {
201                    pthread_join(threads[i] , NULL);
202            }
```

```
203          //Free our now joined threads.
204          free(threads);
205 }
206 void* compute_cells(void* args) {
207          struct thread_args* thread_args = (struct thread_args*) args;
208          bool** ib = thread_args->ib;
209          bool** cb = thread_args->cb;
210          struct simple_barrier* barrier = thread_args->barrier;
211
212          //Add one to each row calculation to account for our grid
             boarders.
213          int start_row = thread_args->start_row;
214          int end_row = thread_args->end_row;
215
216          for (int itr = 0; itr < g_iterations; itr++) {
217                  for (int i = start_row; i <= end_row; i++) {
218                          for (int j = 1; j <= g_columns; j++) {
219                                  compute_cell(i, j, ib, cb);
220                          }
221                  }
222
223                  //Swap boards.
224                  bool** tmp = cb;
225                  cb = ib;
226                  ib = tmp;
227
228                  //Syncronize between iterations.
229                  simple_barrier_wait(barrier);
230
231                  if (g_display) {
232                          //The first thread can handle the printing in the
    case of display mode.
233                          if (start_row == 1) {
234                                  print_board(ib, g_rows, g_columns);
235                                  sleep(1);
236                          }
237                  }
238          }
239 }
240
241 void compute_cell(int r, int c, bool** ib, bool** cb) {
242          int value = ib[r-1][c-1] + ib[r][c-1] + ib[r+1][c-1]
243                  + ib[r-1][ c] + ib[r+1][c]
244                  + ib[r-1][c+1] + ib[r][c+1] + ib[r+1][c+1] ;
245
246          if (value == 3 || (ib[r][c] && value == 2)) {
247                  cb[r][c] = true;
248          } else {
249                  cb[r][c] = false;
250          }
```

```
251          return;
252 }
253
254 void compute_whole_board(bool ** initial_board, bool **
      computed_board, int width, int height) {
255
256          for (int i = 1; i <= height; i++) {
257
258                  for (int j = 1; j <= width; j++) {
259
260                          int value = 0;
261
262                          if (initial_board[i-1][j-1] ) { value++; }
263                          if (initial_board[i][j-1] ) { value++; }
264                          if (initial_board[i+1][j-1] ) { value++; }
265
266                          if (initial_board[i-1][j] ) { value++; }
267                          if (initial_board[i+1][j] ) { value++; }
268
269                          if (initial_board[i-1][j+1] ) { value++; }
270                          if (initial_board[i][j+1] ) { value++; }
271                          if (initial_board[i+1][j+1] ) { value++; }
272
273
274                          if (initial_board[i][j] ) {
275                                  if (value < 2) { computed_board[i][j] =false; }
276                                  if (value == 2 || value == 3)
                                         { computed_board[i][j] = true; }
277                                  if (value > 3) { computed_board[i][j] = false; }
278                          } else {
279                                  if (value == 3) {
280                                          computed_board[i][j] = true;
281                                  } else {
282                                          computed_board[i][j] = false;
283                                  }
284                          }
285                  }
286          }
287 }
```

INDEX

Printed in the United States
By Bookmasters